Time To Care

A Guide to Nursing Home Care in the Upstate

Arnold & Arnold
Attorneys At Law

Contributing Authors:

Andrew Arnold, Brian Arnold, Jodie Fowler

Editor:

Bradley Ridlehoover

ISBN: 1-4033-1077-7 (e-book)
ISBN: 1-4033-1078-5 (Paperback)

This book is printed on acid free paper.

1stBooks - rev. 06/24/02

Table of Contents

Chapter One   The Beginning Steps 1

                        Medical Needs 2

                        Physical and Mental Functioning 3

                        Support Group 5

                        Financial Considerations 5

                        Other Options 7

Chapter Two   Choosing the Right Home 9

Chapter Three   The Warning Signs 13

                        Dehydration 13

                        Bedsores 15

                        Weight-loss 19

                        Under-Staffing 21

Chapter Four   Pain 25

Chapter Five   The Law 30

                        State Law 30

                        Federal Law 31

Appendix 1   Nursing Home General Information 41

Appendix 2   Resident Measures 69

Appendix 3   Inspection Results 75

Appendix 4   Nursing Staff Hours 107

Appendix 5   Ombudsman Contact List 117

Introduction

The greatest responsibility in my nine years of practicing law came this past January when I represented Carrie Berry in her case against a billion-dollar nursing home chain. Mrs. Berry suffered from severe dementia and during the last years of her life had been unable to speak for herself. When she suffered two fractures of her lower left leg (June 1998 and again in August 1998), the nursing home staff ignored her pain. On both occasions Mrs. Berry laid in her bed in the dark for over 24 hours—suffering alone. She was unable to speak for herself. In January 2001, I had the responsibility to tell the jury what had happened to Mrs. Berry.

In fact, although some of the nursing home's staff ignored Mrs. Berry, there was also evidence that the staff did not have *Time To Care*. Staffing levels resulted in about 2 hours of care per day for a resident—and within this time the resident must be bathed, dressed, changed (for the vast majority are incontinent), turned and repositioned every two hours, and perhaps most importantly, fed. Of course, there is still medicine to administer and medical care to deliver. All in two hours! And in this nursing home, one out of three lost more than 10% of their body weight in 180 days.

So, if you get nothing else from this book, get this: It is staffing stupid. You want at least 3 hours of care per day for each resident— and that is rock bottom.

Unfortunately, more than a few residents have harmful experiences in nursing homes. And education can help mitigate a bad experience, but in the end it is up to those providing care to know precisely what it is they are supposed to do and to do it. In those instances in which a nursing home does harm, it really is the responsibility of the family to ensure that all reasonable steps are taken to remedy that wrong and to deter it from happening again. Our firm represents families who have had love ones harmed by the neglect and indifference of some nursing homes.

But thankfully, many nursing homes are properly staffed and provide high levels of care to its residents. It is the goal of this information guide to help the family make a decision on the front end and to find the highest level of care for their loved one.

Chapter One

The Beginning Steps

Nobody wants to put Grandma in the nursing home. And probably for good reason: Many nursing homes are not prepared to provide the types of basic personal and medical services necessary for maximum health. And even when Grandma is put in a "good" nursing home, the loss of independence and the depression that follows can be devastating. And men who have spent their entire lives as bread winners and the "man of the house" can simply fall apart when put in a nursing home.

In fact other options exist (discussed briefly below); but sometimes there really is very little choice in the matter. And putting Grandma in the nursing home does not mean that you will be doing nothing: Quite the opposite. You must be diligent. Watch. Ask questions. Be alert. Maybe even raise your voice. You have a role to play.

And the first role is to determine the need for placement in a long-term care facility (i.e., nursing home). You must make sure that a thorough assessment is done of all the individual's care needs and capabilities. Assessing the need for institutional placement must include an evaluation of the medical needs, and also the physical and mental functioning of the individual as well as social support (friends and family). And do not forget about financial issues.

Medical Needs

First, the individual obviously needs to see a doctor. A doctor can determine the medical problems that require institutional care and advise on rehabilitation, as well as assess the probability of successful treatment and long-term prospects. Sometimes this process can result in treatment of a medical condition and may actually delay the necessity of placement in a nursing home. With this information, a family can determine whether the family and its support groups can weave together a solution or whether the task appears beyond the resources available.

Many times medical conditions are treated with prescription drugs. Elderly folks are more sensitive to drugs, intended as well as unintended. It is not uncommon for someone in his 70's to be on 9 or 10 prescriptions. The need to monitor such an individual can be difficult. Also, certain conditions, such as diabetes, require the giving of shots and regular testing of glucose levels. Diabetes requires a close monitoring of the diet.

A doctor can advise on an entire regimen of treatment and dietary strategies. And for those with medical needs requiring full time nursing care a nursing home offers an option. Most nursing homes have a registered dietician on staff. Nursing homes have access to pharmacists and doctors to ensure the proper administration of drugs. Rehabilitation and mental health services are also available. A good nursing home can be a Godsend.

Physical and Mental Functioning

The medical conditions of a person naturally have an impact on their ability to function physically and mentally. Although a physician can throw some light on limitations of mental functioning, some good old fashion common sense can tell you what you need to know about someone's physical abilities. Just watch. What tasks can be performed safely? What activities does she have trouble with? Does she take her medication as prescribed? How much does she eat? How much does she sleep?

Take for an example someone who is already dependent on the family for care is diagnosed with Alzheimer's or other form of dementia. First, if this person is mobile, then concerns about wandering if left alone may dictate twenty-four hour supervision. If the person is immobile, then the notion of her taking care of herself in light of impaired short-term memory does not look good. Taking too much medication or not enough are always possibilities with someone who has dementia.

Incontinence (insufficient bladder and/or bowel control) is also a condition that requires full time care. Most of the time incontinence is coupled with being bed ridden. A person who is incontinent needs to be changed rather frequently.

Many people cannot feed themselves. Weight loss is a clear sign that someone needs assistance eating. And those folks who take prescription medicine can experience a decline in physical and mental functioning. Many times medications can make a person sleep longer than is healthy. Some drugs dampen appetite or increase the intensity of other drugs.

Talk to the doctor about mental functioning and a prognosis for the next twelve months. And pay attention to the actual limitations on functioning caused by her medical conditions. And ask yourself, can she safely do every task necessary to maintain maximum health? If the answer is "no," long term care is a possibility.

Support Group

More clearly stated: Other than you, who else cares? I mean really cares. Who will dedicate a regular amount of time each week to make sure Grandma is taken care of? Who will dedicate a regular financial contribution to pay for the care? Add up all the time for each week and add up all the money. If there are not enough hours from Grandma's support group to take care of her, then a nursing home becomes an option.

But, let's be clear. When the resources of the support group will allow Grandma to stay out of a nursing home, then keep her out!

Financial Considerations

Who is going to pay for all of this? Good question.

First, you can expect to pay between $3000 and $6000 a month for nursing home care. Medicare and Medicaid may pay for some of it. But, Medicare usually only covers nursing home admissions that follow a hospital stay, and then are limited to 60 days. Some Medicare supplemental insurance plans ("Medigap") cover nursing home care, but only when that care is covered by Medicare.

Medicaid is a state and federal program that pay only for people with limited income and assets. Medicaid is the primary payer for about 7 out of 10 nursing home residents. If Grandma owns a house, then Medicaid is probably not an option. And before you think about just getting rid of the house and giving the money to the grandchildren, there are a host of legal issues. Do not do this without talking to an attorney.

It is entirely possible, that Grandma's savings might need to be used to pay for some or all of her care. Also, it is possible to get a "reverse mortgage" which gives a homeowner regular monthly income up to the equity of the home.

Long-term care insurance is relatively new. The National Association of Insurance Commissioners (NAIC) has a free publication called "A Shopper's Guide to Long-Term Care Insurance. Also, Medicare has a publication, Guide to Health Insurance for People with Medicare, which can be obtained by calling 1-800-MEDICARE. Although it will not help much now, for those who can plan many years in advance can really make things easier on themselves and their loved ones. So, after you figure out how to pay for Grandma's nursing home care, check into long-term care insurance so that your children will not be faced with some heart-wrenching choices.

Other Options

To be quite honest, there does not seem to be any really good options. The new trend of adult day care is just that—a trend. It is not materialized as an option in many locales.

The South Carolina Department of Health and Human Services offers access to the most information about local options. For example, respite programs are intended to allow families to keep Grandma at home as long as possible while also recognizing the demands on the caregivers and their families. Respite means a short break from the demands of care giving. Essentially, a group home would allow a caregiver to drop Grandma off for a few hours to allow a rest for the caregiver. This could be done at regular intervals so as to take the stress off home life. Also, there are some programs designed for folks with Alzheimer's. Contact the S.C. Department of Health and Human Services by calling (803) 898-2850.

Assisted living communities are an option for those who require some monitoring, accessible medical services, and laundry and meals service. Some of these communities are very nice and just as many are very expensive. But for those who want to retain some independence and are able to do so, an assisted living facility may be an option.

Home and community care programs can offer assistance. Meals-on-Wheels is an example of a community program that might be just one piece of multi-faceted plan to allow Grandma to stay at home. Charities like the United Way have a list of community programs that might help you.

Also, try Geriatric Resource Services, Inc. (864) 297-1336. A geriatric care manager can help you with getting a plan and piecing together options.

Chapter Two

Choosing the Right Home

When a thorough assessment of Grandma's medical needs, physical and mental functioning, the financial resources, the support group and all of your options suggest that a nursing home is a necessity, then the hard part starts: What nursing home?

Not all nursing homes are created equal. Some are properly staffed with competent and caring nurses and nursing assistants. Many are warehouses designed to minimize expenditures of staffing to maximize the bottom line. Your job is to be able to tell the difference and find one that will take care of Grandma.

You need to evaluate the following factors:

1. **Availability**

    This might sound obvious but nursing homes have a limited number of beds, and even less beds for Medicaid or Medicare patients. Current cutbacks in our State's Medicaid budget will not help matters. So, make sure you realize that availability is limited, and you might want to check out some waiting lists as soon as possible.

2. **Location**

This is critical. You want a nursing home close enough so that you can pop in often and at a moment's notice. You want a nursing home close to the maximum number of family and friends, so all can visit and visit often.

3. **Staffing**

Adequate nurse staffing is critical to the delivery of quality patient care. The Joint Commission on Accreditation of Healthcare Organization's (JCAHO) Standards for Long-Term Care states "negative outcomes frequently result from inadequate number of staff." Staffing is so important that I would prefer a nursing home 20 or 30 miles further out for higher staffing levels.

[see detailed discussion on Staffing in Chapter 3]

4. **Inspection results**

Nursing homes are required to be licensed, and are required to submit to annual inspections (actually the inspections occur anywhere from every 9 to 15 months). These inspections look at the quality of care, staffing, resident assessment, nutrition and dietary deficiencies, and record keeping. The average nursing home in this state has 7 deficiencies.

Inspections (latest inspection results are in the Appendix in the back of this book) will indicate what the specific deficiency was, the date of correction, the level of harm (scale 1 to 4) and the number of residents affected. Also, at www.medicare.gov, use "Nursing Home Care" to get even more up to date inspections. Finally, look at the last three inspections. What is the average number of deficiencies for that time period? Is there a trend?

Clearly, you want a nursing home that has no more than an average of 7 deficiencies over the last three years with low levels of harm that affected only a few or some residents. You would also like to see a trend toward improving care.

5. **Call an Ombudsman**

Ombudsmen are state sponsored advocates for the elderly who investigate allegations of abuse and/or neglect of the elderly. Ombudsmen are a very good source of information and are willing to discuss the latest inspection results with you as well as provide you with information about a nursing home's complaint history.

In the back of the book is a list of Ombudsmen who serve the upstate.

6. **Ask Around**

You would be surprised how many people know someone who knows someone who knows something helpful. Word of mouth can be the most reliable source of information about a nursing home. Pay attention to the paper for any reports about a particular nursing home or any lawsuits involving a local nursing home.

Also, local advocacy groups can be a great source of information. The Association for Protection of the Elderly in Lexington, SC is one I highly recommend. (Go to www.apeape.org.)

Chapter Three

The Warning Signs

A buse and neglect in nursing homes come in many forms and manifest itself in many ways. Although there are many warning signs of abuse and neglect, such as bone fractures, depression, bruising, infections, inadequate hygiene, unclean living conditions, and unexplained accidents, the following are the most common and prevalent warning signs.

Dehydration:

Hydration is critical to health, particularly of the elderly and failure to properly hydrate residents can be an obvious sign of neglect.

The elderly are at a higher risk of dehydration than others for two main reasons: reduced fluid intake and increased fluid loss. These are caused by various factors—altered thirst sensation, greater use of medication, more disease processes, and less ability to hydrate themselves. Thus, nursing homes should make proper hydration, as well as detection of dehydration, a primary goal.

Proper hydration, thus the prevention of dehydration, requires care, planning, close attention to the residents, and common sense. Prevention can be simple:

- Increase fluids at mealtime
- Increase fluids while taking medication
- Take necessary precautions against illnesses, such as the flu, that may cause fluid loss
- Maintain proper humidity

If a resident becomes dehydrated, detection is often based upon an imperfect and crude evaluation of the resident. Warning signs and symptoms of dehydration include headaches, fatigue, dizziness, dark urine, difficulty in swallowing, painful urination, and delirium. A dietician or doctor may also consider the resident's appetite, frequency of medications, and body weight. If dehydration is suspected, the nursing home has a responsibility to act quickly. Lab work should be performed and proper medical treatment should be implemented-IV fluid intake with proper sodium levels.

There are three types of dehydration:

1. Isotonic: a balanced loss of water and sodium.
2. Hypertonic: loss of more water than sodium.
3. Hypotonic: loss of more sodium than water.

Each type requires a slightly different approach to treatment.

The seriousness of dehydration lies not in the symptoms listed above but in the problematic health conditions it can cause or aggravate. Among these conditions are kidney stone formation, bedsores, respiratory sickness, diabetes complications, infections (urinary tract is common), and some types of cancer.

Because the elderly are already more prone to illness, dehydration only increases such chances of illnesses as it weakens the overall body. If dehydration is not quickly and properly treated, it can be fatal. There is no excuse for a resident becoming dehydrated and certainly no excuse for not detecting it and properly treating it.

Bedsores:

Bedsores, or pressure ulcers as they are sometimes called, are a serious and unfortunate common occurrence among residents in nursing homes. This is so because the most significant risk factor of developing a bedsore is immobility—someone who cannot move or get out of bed on their own and must depend on the care of another. Because most bedsores are preventable, the mere existence of one may indicate a failure by the nursing home to properly reposition a resident, among other failures.

In short, a bedsore is caused by unrelieved pressure on the skin that results in damage to the underlying skin tissue. There are four stages of bedsores.

Stage I is an observable redness (alteration of skin) caused by pressure.

Stage II is an observable thinning of a skin area and appears as a blister or abrasion.

Stage III is an observable thinning and skin loss with damage to the underlying tissue and appears as a deep crater or blister.

Stage IV is a full skin loss with extensive damage to the skin and underlying tissue, involving necrosis (rotting of skin) and may cause damage to the muscle and bone.

When someone is first admitted to a nursing home, the nursing home should perform a full evaluation of the resident to determine the existence of any risk factors for developing a bedsore. The following are a number of risk factors that should be considered by a nursing home when caring for a resident to prevent a bedsore:

a. Immobility-confined to bed or a chair.

b. Inability to turn or reposition oneself.

c. Poor or inadequate nutrition and hydration.

d. Altered level of consciousness.

e. Medical condition that may cause weakening of the skin.

If a resident has one or more of these risk factors, the nursing home should take proper steps to prevent the development of bedsores. Having these risk factors does not excuse the nursing home if a bedsore develops, it only means the nursing home should provide additional care to prevent them.

To prevent the development of bedsores in an at-risk resident, there are many steps that should be taken:

a. Turn and reposition the resident a minimum of every two hours so that the pressure on the skin is relieved.

b. Inspection of the skin at least once daily for evidence of any redness.

c. Reduce the elevation of the head of the bed to reduce friction-the resident sliding down in the bed.

d. Keep the skin dry and clean.

e. Make sure the resident has proper nutrition-adequate calorie and protein intake. This helps the skin get nourishment and stay healthy.

f. Activity. The nursing home should attempt to improve the mobility of the resident.

g. Use of an air mattress or other specialized bed helps reduce pressure to the areas of the skin that receives the most pressure.

These steps are fundamental and should be taken by the nursing home. Existence of a bedsore usually means one or more of the above steps were not followed by the nursing home.

And if after all precaution and necessary steps are taken, a resident develops a bedsore, which is doubtful, the nursing home has a responsibility to take an active and aggressive approach to healing the bedsore.

The most important part of healing a bedsore is early detection. This should be accomplished if the nursing performed the daily skin inspection. If a bedsore is not detected until Stage II or later, this is an indication that the daily skin inspections were likely not taking place.

After detection of a bedsore, a review of the resident's charts should be made to identify what caused the bedsore. At that time, all caregivers (dietician, doctor, nurse, and CNA) should be consulted to develop a care plan to promote healing of the bedsore. The dietician should make sure the resident has proper nutrition and to adopt a diet that promotes the healing of the bedsores and nourish the skin. A re-evaluation should be made of the care plan if the bedsore is not healing.

Bedsores are arguably the most serious problems facing residents in nursing homes today. Unfortunately, because most can be prevented, this means that nursing homes are simply not caring for the residents in most of these bedsore incidents (the section below on staffing illustrates how the necessary care is not being provided).

Weight-loss:

Malnutrition is the silent epidemic in our nursing homes. Studies have shown that from 35 to 85 percent of nursing home residents in the United States are malnourished. The effects of malnutrition are devastating. Malnutrition can lead to infections, bedsores, slow healing, bones fractures, and fatigue.

Adequate nutrition is essential for health and life. Yet malnutrition is common in nursing homes. Most of the time, it is avoidable. The reason for such malnutrition is simple: the residents are not getting the proper amount of calories and protein.

One of the most significant causes of this is understaffing. It takes 30 to 60 minutes to feed a resident, who cannot feed themselves, safely and adequately. However, as shown in the section below on understaffing, nursing homes simply do not employ enough staff to feed and nourish its residents. This means that food is either placed in front of a resident and eating was up to them or the staff feeds the residents quickly and forcefully. In either event, the nursing home is not providing proper and adequate care.

Prevention of malnutrition is simple in most circumstances-take the time and care to feed the resident. Further, when weight-loss occurs, or the resident refuses to eat, supplements should be ordered by the doctor and administered by the nursing home.

The consequences of malnutrition in the elderly are serious, as detailed above. Malnutrition leads to a decrease in a resident's quality of life, health, and happiness. Unfortunately, the malnourished residents in nursing homes are being deprived of one of life's great pleasures, as well as essentials—food.

Under-Staffing:

An underlying and prevalent cause of many injuries, such as the dehydration, bedsores, and weight-loss, sustained by residents of nursing homes is understaffing. This simply means there are not enough qualified personnel in a nursing home to properly care for all the residents.

The primary caregiver of residents at nursing homes, meaning the one who performs most of if not all the tasks needed to take proper care of the resident, is a certified nursing assistant ("CNA"). To understand how understaffing occurs consider that a CNA typically works an 7.5-hour shift, but with two 15 minute breaks and a 30-minute meal, the CNA only has 6.5 hours of actual time to care for the residents. This allows for 390 minutes for resident care in each shift.

Now consider the minutes required for a CNA to complete the responsibilities and tasks that he or she may have on a single shift when responsible for 9 residents (unfortunately CNAs are commonly responsible for 12 to 15 residents on a shift):

1. 4 showers to give   60 min.
2. 5 baths   75 min.

3.	5 incontinent residents to clean/change	25 min.
4.	One catheter to empty	5 min.
5.	Document on the resident care charts throughout shift	25 min.
6.	Change 9 bed sheets and make up beds	40 min.
7.	Turn/ reposition 4 bed-ridden residents every 2 hours	60 min.
8.	Set up 6 meals	25 min.
9.	Toilet 4 to 6 residents 2 times a shift	60 min.
10.	Shave/groom/hygiene all residents	135 min.
TOTAL MINUTES TO PROVIDE CARE:		**510 MIN.**

Therefore, a CNA with only 9 residents would need approximately 510 minutes to complete these tasks to adequately care for the residents. Yet, the CNA only works for a total of 390 minutes. Thus, the CNA would need 120 more minutes, or two additional hours of non-stop work, to perform the resident care responsibilities. This is if the CNA works diligently during the 390 minutes. However, many CNAs work a double shift at the facility or have another job at another nursing home, hold down two jobs due to low wages- resulting in many days of sixteen-hour workdays, and often work six or seven days per week. Meaning these 390 minutes are likely to be less than productive.

Thus, when pushed for time, a CNA will shave some time off feedings. Those who do not eat quickly will miss some calories.

Over a period of time, the calories add up and an elderly person in need of all of their calories to fight off infections and to heal will begin to lose weight, develop infections, and pressure sores.

Also, instead of checking, changing, turning, and repositioning residents, they skip a turn or two. This leads to the deterioration of the skin and the development of rashes (fungal and bacteria infections) and bedsores. Fungal and bacterial infections can get into the blood stream and cause serious illness, even death. Bedsores are painful and just as dangerous.

Simply put: much of the care needed to ensure the residents are safe and healthy is neglected because the CNA cannot perform the work by her or himself.

An accurate calculation of a facility's staffing needs can be complex. It requires an assessment of the specific needs of that facility's residents (for example the more residents who are incontinent and suffer from dementia the greater number of staff needed to provide adequate care). But there are a few good rules of thumbs: there should be a minimum of 1 nurse per shift per 20 residents and the "average" resident needs at least 3 hours of CNA care per day. To calculate hours of CNA care per day, take the number of CNAs that work on that day, multiply by 7 (hours) and divide by the number of residents. This is the hours per patient day of care for each resident. It should be at least equal to 3 hours.

At the back of this book we have staffing information for most upstate nursing homes. This information is available at www.medicare.gov. Click on "Nursing Home Compare." Use the information about a nursing home's residents (such as number with incontinence) to see if the resident mix is one that will stretch the demands of the staff compared with other nursing homes under consideration.

Chapter Four

Pain

Pain is defined as "an unpleasant sensation, occurring in varying degrees of severity as a consequence of injury, disease, or emotional disorder." Pain is a common and treatable condition among the elderly. Even though pain is a familiar ailment of the elderly, it is not normal. Unfortunately, many assume that pain is just a normal part of growing old and consequently pain suffered by the elderly is frequently ignored, unnoticed or under treated. **Pain can be one of the most exhausting and overwhelming side effects of aging.** If pain is left untreated it can lead to depression and poor self-esteem and can affect the quality of life.

Recent studies show that severe pain among nursing home residents is prevalent, persistent and poorly treated. Our ability to recognize pain suffered by a loved one, monitor the treatment of the pain and understand the full range of consequences of pain will make us better able to protect those we love.

An expert in forensic psychiatry, pain management and pain medicine explained to me that an individual with severe dementia (such as Alzheimer's) cannot reason through their pain. Pain torments those with dementia. The expert further explained that an individual with dementia who experiences pain also experiences fear and anxiety. Fear and anxiety lower the threshold of pain thereby increasing the sensation of pain felt by those with dementia. The increased sensation of pain increases fear and anxiety, which in turn lowers the threshold of pain…creating a vicious cycle of suffering.

Sometimes the best indicator of pain is what the person says or expresses. The person with pain is the expert about his or her pain. Recognizing pain in people who experience cognitive impairment can be a matter of noticing differences in their behavior. There is no test or exam for pain and people respond differently to pain. People express pain in different ways: some cry out, some stay still, some try to bear pain without showing it, some frown and some look sad.

During one study, researchers videotaped the facial expressions of participants during a procedure. The people with dementia were five times more likely to use facial expressions than cognitively normal patients. The study concluded that even though people with dementia did not show the same response as people who were cognitively intact, both their behavioral and physiologic responses indicate they were feeling pain. Thus, increased heart rate, confusion, anger and irritability might signal underlying pain that is not being treated appropriately.

Pain management is the systematic study of clinical and basic science and its application for the reduction of pain and suffering. Pain management is a newly emerging discipline with a goal of reducing pain.

There are some reasons why pain management in the elderly is considered tricky business. First, elderly people usually have multiple medical problems and a determination has to be made as to which health problem is causing the pain. Memory impairment can also create a problem in pain management. Additionally, there is an increased possibility of side effects of medications in the elderly. However, these problems should never hinder the proper assessment, treatment and management of pain. Pain should be treated wisely, appropriately and aggressively.

A "team approach" to managing pain in a long-term care facility works well. First, the administrator of the facility should establish a "team approach". The administrator is also the person at the facility who is responsible for enforcing the appropriate state and federal rules and regulations. Second, the nursing supervisor should oversee the pain management plan and should educate the staff properly about the pain management plan for the individual patient. Finally, the nurses must carry out the pain management plan and observe the patient.

The primary caregivers, who work closely with the residents helping them do all the activities of daily living, should be able to identify when someone is in pain. While nursing assistants do not administer pain medication, they are usually the primary caregivers in this setting, providing 90 percent of the direct care in nursing homes. But if the caregivers do not recognize pain in the resident, there is a breakdown in system of effectively managing pain.

Nursing home staff more often than not underestimate the pain that the residents experience. A solution to the problem of nursing home staff underestimating pain would be to educate nursing home staff, especially the nursing assistants who are typically the least trained, so that they might better identify pain and manage pain. It takes an attentive and enduring caregiver to notice pain, observe the trial of treatment and relieve pain. Pain needs constant reassessment. Pain assessment in nursing homes should be the "fifth vital sign", regularly checked.

Because nursing home staff often underestimate the pain that residents experience, you should be leery of studies and research resulting from data collected by nursing home staff. The Minimum Data Set (MDS) is a nationally mandated nursing home resident assessment instrument, which is used to collect details on residents including assessing pain symptoms. In December 2000, the Inspector General (IG) of the US Department of Health and Human Services issued a report wherein it suggested that the MDS document and the process are flawed. The Inspector General recommended that the Health Care Financing Administration work with the nursing home industry to provide enhanced and coordinated training to nursing homes.

Here are some questions you can ask to help determine if a facility may be treating pain adequately: Does the facility require periodic assessments of possible pain? When potential pain is identified, does anyone respond? Does the response to serious pain include opiate drugs on a regular schedule?

I would suggest that family members inquire about the pain assessment, treatment and management policies practiced by the nursing home or long-term care facility. I would also recommend that the family get involved as much as possible in the pain management plan of their loved one. You as a family member should be a strong advocate for your loved one to ensure that they receive proper and adequate pain relief.

Chapter Five

The Law

There are many laws and regulations that protect residents of nursing homes, often referred to as long-term care nursing homes. Much of the protection is based upon federal law: The Federal Nursing Home Reform Law which was passed in 1987 provided very specific and broad protections for residents of nursing homes. State law, including the South Carolina Bill of Rights for Residents of Long-Term Care Nursing homes and an elder abuse statute, combined with common law remedies for negligence offer residents additional protections.

State Law

South Carolina has laws designed to protect nursing home residents. It is a crime in South Carolina to abuse or neglect any vulnerable adult. The State ombudsman office is mandated to investigate allegations of abuse and neglect that occur in nursing homes. Sometimes law enforcement becomes involved and criminally prosecutes individuals for abuse and neglect.

State common law provides remedies for residents who are harmed by neglect and abuse. A resident injured by poor medical care, lack of medical attention, poor dietary services, or other actions of an employee of a nursing home may seek a remedy for the harm in court. A resident is entitled to compensation for medical bills, pain and suffering, wrongful death and other physical injuries caused by nursing home staff. In severe cases, punitive damages may be available.

Federal Law

Federal laws and regulations provide the most specific forms of protection for residents of nursing homes. The federal law was enacted in order to "promote and protect the rights of each resident." In order for nursing homes to be a part of the Medicare or Medicaid programs, they have to meet the following requirements:

Accommodation of Needs

Nursing home residents must receive reasonable accommodations of their needs and preferences.

Activities

Nursing homes must provide social activities that reflect the interests of the nursing home residents. Normally provision for activities should be made in the plan of care for each resident.

Admission Policy

No facility may require a third party guarantee of payment or accept any gifts as a condition of residence staying there. They may accept contributions to their facility only if they do not influence admission or continued stay.

Nursing homes may not require residents to waive their right to receive or apply for Medicare or Medicaid benefits.

Facility may charge those residents who are Medicaid-eligible for requested services or items.

Care Plan

A team of nurses, social workers, nutritionist and other therapists must design a care plan which attempts to address all the residents care needs. A resident must be assessed for risk of pressure sores, falls, pain, and harmful drug interactions. A resident must be monitored and any changes must be taken into account in the resident's plan of care.

Choice

Residents have the right to choose their own physician(s).

Residents should be permitted to participate in their own care and treatment.

Dignity

Individual residents will be treated with dignity and respect by the facility and their staff.

Exercise of Rights

Nursing home residents have the freedom to exercise their rights as residents without fear of discrimination, restraint, interference, coercion or reprisal.

Grievances

Grievances may be voiced without fear of discrimination or reprisal. The nursing home must resolve grievances promptly.

Quality of Life

Nursing homes must provide a level of care that enhances the quality of life.

Mail

Nursing homes will promptly send and receive resident mail unopened. Residents will have access to writing materials and supplies.

Notice of Bed-Hold Policy

Family members and residents are to receive written notice of state and facility bed-hold policies before and at the time of a transfer.

Notice of Rights and Services

Residents should receive information (in writing and orally) of all of their rights, the applicable rules, and all regulations regarding conduct and responsibilities.

Residents have the right to refuse medical treatment.

Residence may inspect and purchase duplicate copies of their health records.

Nursing homes are obligated to keep residents up-to-date and informed as to their state of health.

Residents may refuse room changes that are requested by the facility.

Residents will be notified of their Medicare and Medicaid benefits. This will be accessible in an appropriate location.

A facility must inform residents of applicable services and charges.

The facility will notify their residents and interested family members of room or roommate changes.

A facility must notify its residents or certain family members of any changes in the rights provided.

Participation in Resident Groups

Residents may participate in any groups that do not violate any laws.

Nursing homes need to provide appropriate spaces for groups and meetings.

If invited by a group or meeting, staff and others may attend the meeting.

A nursing home facility will adequately address any concerns of a group.

Participation in Other Activities

Residents can participate in any activities as long as they do not violate the rights of other residents.

Property

Residents are permitted to retain and use their own personal property as they desire provided that the space is available.

Protection of Funds

Residents may handle their own finances.

Any funds that are deposited to the facility will be handled with the best interests of the depositor.

Deposited funds with the facility will be protected by a security bond.

Deposited funds will not be intermixed with the funds of the facility.

Upon request, the facility must provide a quarterly, personalized financial report.

Restraints

Nursing homes are not allowed to use physical restraints, nor are they allowed to use psychoactive drugs, on residence for either discipline or as a simple convenience. These can only be used if they are for the purpose of treating legitimate medical purposes.

Right of Privacy

Residents have the right of privacy, which includes:

- Personal care
- Medical treatments and Medical Records
- Telephone use
- Visits

- Personal Correspondence
- Family or group meetings

Social Services

Nursing homes must provide those social services that protect or bolster resident's well being.

Staff Treatment

Nursing homes must protect its residents from staff abuse and neglect.

If staff abuse or neglect is suspected or alleged, nursing homes must investigate the incident and report it to the state ombudsman or appropriate state agency (DHEC).

Telephone

Residents must be allowed to use the telephone in private.

Transfer and Discharge

Transfers and discharges is permitted when the nursing home cannot meet the specific needs of a resident or if it necessary to protect the safety of a resident.

In addition, transfers and discharges may occur when the resident no longer needs long-term care services or is unable to make the proper payments.

Nursing homes must provide residents with safe transfers or a discharge.

Residential Environment

Nursing homes must provide an environment that is safe, clean, comfortable, and as close to a normal home as is reasonable. This includes ensuring that residences have clean and adequate baths and as well as clean bed linens.

Nursing homes must provide housekeeping and maintenance services.

Lighting and sound must be maintained at adequate and comfortable levels.

Nursing homes will maintain comfortable and safe temperature levels.

Visitation Rights

Residents may receive or deny visitors.

Nursing homes must allow visitation rights with any state or federal agency that provides health, social, or legal services.

Work

Residents cannot be forced to work or perform services for the facility. And any resident who choose to work for the nursing home must be paid. The nursing home must also keep detail records of the type of work performed.

Arnold & Arnold, Attorneys at Law

Appendix 1

Nursing Home General Information

(All information was obtained from the Nursing Home Compare Info at www.medicare.gov. This website is produced by **Centers for Medicare & Medicaid Services** 7500 Security Boulevard, Baltimore MD 21244-1850 Phone: 410-786-3000)

Abbeville County

Abbeville Nursing Home
P.O. Box 190
Abbeville, SC 29620
(864) 459-5122

Number of Beds: 94
Percentage of Beds Occupied: 96%
Medicare Participation: Yes
Medicaid Participation: Yes
Type of Ownership: For-Profit Corporation
Located Within A Hospital:No
Multi-Nursing Home (chain) Ownership: No
Resident and Family Councils: Both

Anderson County

Anderson Area Medical Center Subacute
800 N. Fant St.
Anderson, SC 29621
(864) 261-1710

Number of Beds:27
Percentage of Beds Occupied: 85%
Medicare Participation: Yes
Medicaid Participation: No
Type of Ownership: Non-Profit Corporation
Located Within A Hospital: Yes
Multi-Nursing Home (chain) Ownership: No
Resident and Family Councils: None

Brookside Nursing Center
208 James St.
Anderson, SC 29625
(864) 226-3427

Number of Beds:88
Percentage of Beds Occupied: 97%
Medicare Participation: Yes
Medicaid Participation: Yes
Type of Ownership: For-Profit Corporation
Located Within A Hospital: No
Multi-Nursing Home (chain) Ownership: Yes
Resident and Family Councils: Both

Ellenburg Nursing Center Inc.
611 E Hampton St.
Anderson, SC 29624
(864) 226-5054

Number of Beds:181
Percentage of Beds Occupied: 97%
Medicare Participation: Yes
Medicaid Participation: Yes
Type of Ownership: For-Profit Corporation
Located Within A Hospital: No
Multi-Nursing Home (chain) Ownership: No
Resident and Family Councils: Both

NHC Healthcare – Anderson
1501 E Greenville St.
P.O. Box 1327
Anderson, SC 29622
(864) 226-8356

Number of Beds:290
Percentage of Beds Occupied: 67%
Medicare Participation: Yes
Medicaid Participation: Yes
Type of Ownership: For-Profit Corporation
Located Within A Hospital: No
Multi-Nursing Home (chain) Ownership: Yes
Resident and Family Councils: Both

Richard M. Campbell Veterans Nursing Home
4605 Belton Hwy
Anderson, SC 29621
(864) 261-6734

Number of Beds:220
Percentage of Beds Occupied: 95%
Medicare Participation: Yes
Medicaid Participation: Yes
Type of Ownership: Government - State
Located Within A Hospital: No
Multi-Nursing Home (chain) Ownership: No
Resident and Family Councils: Both

Willow Creek Nursing Center
406 West Broad St, Box 1119
Iva, SC 29655
(864) 348-7433

Number of Beds:60
Percentage of Beds Occupied: 95%
Medicare Participation: Yes
Medicaid Participation: Yes
Type of Ownership: For-Profit Corporation
Located Within A Hospital: No
Multi-Nursing Home (chain) Ownership: Yes
Resident and Family Councils: Both

Cherokee County

Brookview Healthcare Center
510 Thompson St.
Box 1240
Gaffney, SC 29340
(864) 489-3101

Number of Beds:132
Percentage of Beds Occupied: 98%
Medicare Participation: Yes
Medicaid Participation: Yes
Type of Ownership: For-Profit Corporation
Located Within A Hospital: No
Multi-Nursing Home (chain) Ownership: Yes
Resident and Family Councils: Resident

Cherokee County LTC Facility
1434 N. Limestone St.
Gaffney, SC 29340
(864) 487-2717

Number of Beds:85
Percentage of Beds Occupied: 100%
Medicare Participation: Yes
Medicaid Participation: Yes
Type of Ownership: Government - County
Located Within A Hospital: No
Multi-Nursing Home (chain) Ownership: No
Resident and Family Councils: Both

Chester County

Chester County Nursing Center
1 Medical Park Drive Box 56
Chester, SC 29706
(803) 581-3151

Number of Beds:100
Percentage of Beds Occupied: 100%
Medicare Participation: Yes
Medicaid Participation: Yes
Type of Ownership: Government - County
Located Within A Hospital: Yes
Multi-Nursing Home (chain) Ownership: No
Resident and Family Councils: Both

Fairfield County

Fairfield Homes Inc.
117 Bellfield Road
Ridgeway, SC 29130
(803) 337-2257

Number of Beds:112
Percentage of Beds Occupied: 95%
Medicare Participation: Yes
Medicaid Participation: Yes
Type of Ownership: For-Profit Corporation
Located Within A Hospital: No
Multi-Nursing Home (chain) Ownership: Yes
Resident and Family Councils: Resident

Tanglewood Healthcare Center
Third Street Box 68
Ridgeway, SC 29130
(803) 337-3211

Number of Beds:150
Percentage of Beds Occupied: 91%
Medicare Participation: Yes
Medicaid Participation: Yes
Type of Ownership: For-Profit Corporation
Located Within A Hospital: No
Multi-Nursing Home (chain) Ownership: Yes
Resident and Family Councils: Resident

Greenville County

Allen Bennett Memorial Hospital
313 Memorial Drive
Greer, SC 29651
(864) 848-8500

Number of Beds:10
Percentage of Beds Occupied: 100%
Medicare Participation: Yes
Medicaid Participation: No
Type of Ownership: Non Profit - Other
Located Within A Hospital: Yes
Multi-Nursing Home (chain) Ownership: Yes
Resident and Family Councils: Both

Briarwood Nursing Center
721 W Curtis St.
Simpsonville, SC 29681
(864) 967-7191

Number of Beds:42
Percentage of Beds Occupied: 90%
Medicare Participation: Yes
Medicaid Participation: Yes
Type of Ownership: For-Profit Corporation
Located Within A Hospital: No
Multi-Nursing Home (chain) Ownership: Yes
Resident and Family Councils: Both

Brighton Gardens of Greenville
1306 Pelham Road
Greenville, SC 29615
(864) 286-6600

Number of Beds:45
Percentage of Beds Occupied: 16%
Medicare Participation: Yes
Medicaid Participation: No
Type of Ownership: For-Profit Corporation
Located Within A Hospital: No
Multi-Nursing Home (chain) Ownership: Yes
Resident and Family Councils: Both

Fountain Inn Nursing Home
501 Gulliver St.
P.O. Box 67
Fountain Inn, SC 29644
(864) 862-2554

Number of Beds:44
Percentage of Beds Occupied: 98%
Medicare Participation: Yes
Medicaid Participation: Yes
Type of Ownership: For-Profit Corporation
Located Within A Hospital: No
Multi-Nursing Home (chain) Ownership: Yes
Resident and Family Councils: Both

Greenville Memorial Medical Center Subacute Unit
701 Grove Road
Greenville, SC 29605
(864) 455-7000

Number of Beds:48
Percentage of Beds Occupied: 50%
Medicare Participation: Yes
Medicaid Participation: No
Type of Ownership: Government - State
Located Within A Hospital: Yes
Multi-Nursing Home (chain) Ownership: Yes
Resident and Family Councils: None

Greenville Nursing Center Inc
809 Laurens Road
Greenville, SC 29607
(864) 232-8196

Number of Beds:79
Percentage of Beds Occupied: 97%
Medicare Participation: Yes
Medicaid Participation: Yes
Type of Ownership: For-Profit Corporation
Located Within A Hospital: No
Multi-Nursing Home (chain) Ownership: Yes
Resident and Family Councils: Both

Laurel Baye Healthcare of Greenville
661 Rutherford Road
Greenville, SC 29609
(864) 232-2442

Number of Beds:112
Percentage of Beds Occupied: 100%
Medicare Participation: Yes
Medicaid Participation: Yes
Type of Ownership: For-Profit Corporation
Located Within A Hospital: No
Multi-Nursing Home (chain) Ownership: Yes
Resident and Family Councils: None

Magnolia Manor – Greenville
411 Ansel St.
Greenville, SC 29601
(864) 232-5368

Number of Beds:99
Percentage of Beds Occupied: 89%
Medicare Participation: Yes
Medicaid Participation: Yes
Type of Ownership: For-Profit Corporation
Located Within A Hospital: No
Multi-Nursing Home (chain) Ownership: Yes
Resident and Family Councils: Both

Magnolia Place – Greenville
35 Southpointe Dr.
Greenville, SC 29607
(864) 288-1415

Number of Beds:120
Percentage of Beds Occupied: 90%
Medicare Participation: Yes
Medicaid Participation: Yes
Type of Ownership: For-Profit Corporation
Located Within A Hospital: No
Multi-Nursing Home (chain) Ownership: Yes
Resident and Family Councils: Both

NHC Healthcare – Greenville
1305 Boiling Springs Road
Greer, SC 29650
(864) 458-7566

Number of Beds:176
Percentage of Beds Occupied: 63%
Medicare Participation: Yes
Medicaid Participation: Yes
Type of Ownership: For-Profit Corporation
Located Within A Hospital: No
Multi-Nursing Home (chain) Ownership: Yes
Resident and Family Councils: Resident

NHC Healthcare – Mauldin
850 E Butler Road
Box 600
Mauldin, SC 29662
(864) 675-6421

Number of Beds:120
Percentage of Beds Occupied: 60%
Medicare Participation: Yes
Medicaid Participation: Yes
Type of Ownership: For-Profit Corporation
Located Within A Hospital: No
Multi-Nursing Home (chain) Ownership: No
Resident and Family Councils: Both

Oakmont East – Nursing Center
601 Sulphur Springs Road
Greenville, SC 29611
(864) 246-2721

Number of Beds:132
Percentage of Beds Occupied: 95%
Medicare Participation: Yes
Medicaid Participation: Yes
Type of Ownership: For-Profit Corporation
Located Within A Hospital: No
Multi-Nursing Home (chain) Ownership: Yes
Resident and Family Councils: Resident

Oakmont West Nursing Center
600 Sulphur Springs Road
Greenville, SC 29617
(864) 246-2721

Number of Beds:125
Percentage of Beds Occupied: 96%
Medicare Participation: Yes
Medicaid Participation: Yes
Type of Ownership: For-Profit Corporation
Located Within A Hospital: No
Multi-Nursing Home (chain) Ownership: Yes
Resident and Family Councils: Both

Piedmont Nursing & Rehabilitation Center Inc
401 Chandler Road
Greer, SC 29651
(864) 879-1370

Number of Beds:132
Percentage of Beds Occupied: 95%
Medicare Participation: Yes
Medicaid Participation: Yes
Type of Ownership: For-Profit Corporation
Located Within A Hospital: No
Multi-Nursing Home (chain) Ownership: Yes
Resident and Family Councils: Both

Riverside Nursing Center Inc
109 Bentz Road
Piedmont, SC 29673
(864) 845-5177

Number of Beds:88
Percentage of Beds Occupied: 97%
Medicare Participation: Yes
Medicaid Participation: Yes
Type of Ownership: For-Profit Corporation
Located Within A Hospital: No
Multi-Nursing Home (chain) Ownership: Yes
Resident and Family Councils: Both

Roger Huntington Nursing Center
313 Memorial Drive
Greer, SC 29650
(864) 848-8389

Number of Beds:88
Percentage of Beds Occupied: 95%
Medicare Participation: Yes
Medicaid Participation: Yes
Type of Ownership: Non Profit - Other
Located Within A Hospital: No
Multi-Nursing Home (chain) Ownership: Yes
Resident and Family Councils: Both

Rolling Green Village Health Care Facility
1 Hoke Smith Blvd.
Greenville, SC 29615
(864) 987-9800

Number of Beds:44
Percentage of Beds Occupied: 70%
Medicare Participation: Yes
Medicaid Participation: No
Type of Ownership: Non Profit - Other
Located Within A Hospital: No
Multi-Nursing Home (chain) Ownership: No
Resident and Family Councils: Resident

St. Francis Hospital Transitional Care
1 St. Francis Drive
Greenville, SC 29601
(864) 255-1438

Number of Beds:32
Percentage of Beds Occupied: 78%
Medicare Participation: Yes
Medicaid Participation: No
Type of Ownership: Non Profit – Church Related
Located Within A Hospital: Yes
Multi-Nursing Home (chain) Ownership: Yes
Resident and Family Councils: None

Stroud Nursing Home
2906 Geer Hwy
P.O. Box 216
Marietta, SC 29661
(864) 836-6381

Number of Beds:44
Percentage of Beds Occupied: 100%
Medicare Participation: Yes
Medicaid Participation: Yes
Type of Ownership: For-Profit Corporation
Located Within A Hospital: No
Multi-Nursing Home (chain) Ownership: No
Resident and Family Councils: Both

Summit Place, Inc
807 S. E. Main Street
Simpsonville, SC 29681
(864) 963-6069

Number of Beds:132
Percentage of Beds Occupied: 98%
Medicare Participation: Yes
Medicaid Participation: Yes
Type of Ownership: For-Profit Corporation
Located Within A Hospital: No
Multi-Nursing Home (chain) Ownership: Yes
Resident and Family Councils: Resident

Westside Nursing Center, Inc
8 N Texas Ave
Greenville, SC 29611
(864) 295-1331

Number of Beds:132
Percentage of Beds Occupied: 95%
Medicare Participation: Yes
Medicaid Participation: Yes
Type of Ownership: For-Profit Corporation
Located Within A Hospital: No
Multi-Nursing Home (chain) Ownership: Yes
Resident and Family Councils: Resident

Greenwood County

Health Care Center of Wesley Commons
1110 Marshall Rd Box 1203
Greenwood, SC 29646
(864) 227-7250

Number of Beds:102
Percentage of Beds Occupied: 94%
Medicare Participation: Yes
Medicaid Participation: Yes
Type of Ownership: Non Profit – Church Related
Located Within A Hospital: No
Multi-Nursing Home (chain) Ownership: No
Resident and Family Councils: Both

Magnolia Manor – Greenwood
1415 Parkway Dr.
Greenwood, SC 29646
(864) 227-9500

Number of Beds:88
Percentage of Beds Occupied: 95%
Medicare Participation: Yes
Medicaid Participation: Yes
Type of Ownership: For-Profit Corporation
Located Within A Hospital: No
Multi-Nursing Home (chain) Ownership: Yes
Resident and Family Councils: Both

NHC Healthcare – Greenwood
437 E Cambridge St.
P.O. Box 3109
Greenwood, SC 29648
(864) 223-1950

Number of Beds:152
Percentage of Beds Occupied: 95%
Medicare Participation: Yes
Medicaid Participation: Yes
Type of Ownership: For-Profit Corporation
Located Within A Hospital: No
Multi-Nursing Home (chain) Ownership: Yes
Resident and Family Councils: Resident

Self Memorial Hospital TCU
1325 Spring St.
Greenwood, SC 29646
(864) 227-4111

Number of Beds:27
Percentage of Beds Occupied: 37%
Medicare Participation: Yes
Medicaid Participation: No
Type of Ownership: Government - County
Located Within A Hospital: Yes
Multi-Nursing Home (chain) Ownership: No
Resident and Family Councils: None

Lancaster County

Lancaster Convalescent Center Inc
2044 Pageland Hwy Box 1749
Lancaster, SC 29721

Number of Beds:142
Percentage of Beds Occupied:97%
Medicare Participation: Yes
Medicaid Participation: Yes
Type of Ownership: For-Profit Corporation
Located Within A Hospital: No
Multi-Nursing Home (chain) Ownership: Yes
Resident and Family Councils: Both

Springs Memorial Hospital TCU
800 W Meeting St.
Lancaster, SC 29720
(803) 286-1481

Number of Beds:14
Percentage of Beds Occupied: 100%
Medicare Participation: Yes
Medicaid Participation: No
Type of Ownership: For-Profit Corporation
Located Within A Hospital: Yes
Multi-Nursing Home (chain) Ownership: Yes
Resident and Family Councils: Resident

White Oak Manor – Lancaster
253 Craig Manor Road Box 353 MS
Lancaster, SC 29720
(803) 286-1464

Number of Beds:132
Percentage of Beds Occupied: 96%
Medicare Participation: Yes
Medicaid Participation: Yes
Type of Ownership: For-Profit Corporation
Located Within A Hospital: No
Multi-Nursing Home (chain) Ownership: Yes
Resident and Family Councils: Both

Laurens County

Laurens County Hospital SNF
22725 Hwy 76 East
Clinton, SC 29325
(864) 833-9100

Number of Beds:14
Percentage of Beds Occupied: 14%
Medicare Participation: Yes
Medicaid Participation: No
Type of Ownership: Government – Hospital District
Located Within A Hospital: Yes
Multi-Nursing Home (chain) Ownership: No
Resident and Family Councils: None

Martha Franks Baptist Retirement Center
One Martha Franks Dr.
Laurens, SC 29360
(864) 984-4541

Number of Beds: 88
Percentage of Beds Occupied: 33%
Medicare Participation: Yes
Medicaid Participation: Yes
Type of Ownership: Non Profit – Church Related
Located Within A Hospital: No
Multi-Nursing Home (chain) Ownership: Yes
Resident and Family Councils: Resident

NHC Healthcare – Clinton
304 Jacobs Hwy Box 727
Clinton, SC 29325
(864) 833-2550

Number of Beds:131
Percentage of Beds Occupied: 89%
Medicare Participation: Yes
Medicaid Participation: Yes
Type of Ownership: For-Profit Corporation
Located Within A Hospital: No
Multi-Nursing Home (chain) Ownership: Yes
Resident and Family Councils: Both

NHC Healthcare – Laurens
301 Pinehaven St. Ext
Laurens, SC 29360
(864) 984-6584

Number of Beds:176
Percentage of Beds Occupied: 88%
Medicare Participation: Yes
Medicaid Participation: Yes
Type of Ownership: For-Profit Corporation
Located Within A Hospital:No
Multi-Nursing Home (chain) Ownership: No
Resident and Family Councils: Both

McCormick County

McCormick Health Care Center
1 Holiday Road
McCormick, SC 29835
(864) 391-2390

Number of Beds:120
Percentage of Beds Occupied: 99%
Medicare Participation: Yes
Medicaid Participation: Yes
Type of Ownership: Government - County
Located Within A Hospital: No
Multi-Nursing Home (chain) Ownership: No
Resident and Family Councils: Resident

Newberry County

JF Hawkins Nursing Home
1330 Kinard St.
Newberry, SC 29108
(803) 276-2601

Number of Beds:98
Percentage of Beds Occupied: 83%
Medicare Participation: Yes
Medicaid Participation: Yes
Type of Ownership: Non Profit - Corporation
Located Within A Hospital: No
Multi-Nursing Home (chain) Ownership: No
Resident and Family Councils: Resident

Newberry County Memorial Hospital TCU
2669 Kinard St.
Newberry, SC 29108
(803) 876-7570

Number of Beds:12
Percentage of Beds Occupied: 67%
Medicare Participation: Yes
Medicaid Participation: No
Type of Ownership: Government - County
Located Within A Hospital: Yes
Multi-Nursing Home (chain) Ownership: No
Resident and Family Councils: None

White Oak Manor – Newberry
2555 Kinard St., Box 754
Newberry, SC 29108
(803) 276-6060

Number of Beds:146
Percentage of Beds Occupied: 95%
Medicare Participation: Yes
Medicaid Participation: Yes
Type of Ownership: For-Profit Corporation
Located Within A Hospital: No
Multi-Nursing Home (chain) Ownership: Yes
Resident and Family Councils: Resident

Oconee County

Lila Doyle Nursing Care Facility
298 Memorial Drive
Seneca, SC 29678
(864) 855-7675

Number of Beds:79
Percentage of Beds Occupied: 89%
Medicare Participation: Yes
Medicaid Participation: Yes
Type of Ownership: Non Profit - Corporation
Located Within A Hospital: Yes
Multi-Nursing Home (chain) Ownership: No
Resident and Family Councils: Resident

Mariner HC – Seneca
140 Tokeena Rd
Box 189
Seneca, SC 29678
(864) 882-1642

Number of Beds:132
Percentage of Beds Occupied: 99%
Medicare Participation: Yes
Medicaid Participation: Yes
Type of Ownership: For-Profit Corporation
Located Within A Hospital: No
Multi-Nursing Home (chain) Ownership: Yes
Resident and Family Councils: Both

Pickens County

Blue Ridge Nursing Center, Inc
1850 Crestview Road
Easley, SC 29640
(864) 859-3236

Number of Beds:66
Percentage of Beds Occupied: 98%
Medicare Participation: Yes
Medicaid Participation: Yes
Type of Ownership: For-Profit Corporation
Located Within A Hospital: No
Multi-Nursing Home (chain) Ownership: Yes
Resident and Family Councils: Both

Easley Nursing Center, Inc
200 Anne Dr.
Easley, SC 29640
(864) 859-9754

Number of Beds:103
Percentage of Beds Occupied: 94%
Medicare Participation: Yes
Medicaid Participation: Yes
Type of Ownership: For-Profit Corporation
Located Within A Hospital: No
Multi-Nursing Home (chain) Ownership: Yes
Resident and Family Councils: Resident

Harvey's Nursing Home
163 Love & Care Road
Rt 1, Box 160
Six Mile, SC 29682
(864) 868-2307

Number of Beds:44
Percentage of Beds Occupied: 98%
Medicare Participation: Yes
Medicaid Participation: Yes
Type of Ownership: For-Profit Corporation
Located Within A Hospital: No
Multi-Nursing Home (chain) Ownership: Yes
Resident and Family Councils: Both

Laurel Hill, Inc.
716 E. Cedar Rock St.
Pickens, SC 29671
(864) 878-4739

Number of Beds: 80
Percentage of Beds Occupied: 99%
Medicare Participation: Yes
Medicaid Participation: Yes
Type of Ownership: For-Profit Corporation
Located Within A Hospital: No
Multi-Nursing Home (chain) Ownership: Yes
Resident and Family Councils: Both

Rosemond Nursing Center Inc
138 Rosemond Streed Box 895
Pickens, SC 29671
(864) 878-9620

Number of Beds:44
Percentage of Beds Occupied:98%
Medicare Participation: Yes
Medicaid Participation: Yes
Type of Ownership: For-Profit Corporation
Located Within A Hospital: No
Multi-Nursing Home (chain) Ownership: Yes
Resident and Family Councils: Resident

Spartanburg County

Camp Care Inc
59 Blackstock Road
P.O. Box 9
Inman, SC 29349
(864) 472-2028

Number of Beds:88
Percentage of Beds Occupied: 98%
Medicare Participation: Yes
Medicaid Participation: Yes
Type of Ownership: For-Profit Corporation
Located Within A Hospital: No
Multi-Nursing Home (chain) Ownership: Yes
Resident and Family Councils: Both

Golden Age – Inman
82 N Main St.
Inman, SC 29349
(864) 472-6636

Number of Beds:44
Percentage of Beds Occupied: 100%
Medicare Participation: Yes
Medicaid Participation: Yes
Type of Ownership: For-Profit Corporation
Located Within A Hospital: No
Multi-Nursing Home (chain) Ownership: Yes
Resident and Family Councils: Resident

Inman Nursing Home
51 N. Main St
Inman, SC 29349
(864) 472-9370

Number of Beds:40
Percentage of Beds Occupied:93%
Medicare Participation: Yes
Medicaid Participation: Yes
Type of Ownership: For-Profit Corporation
Located Within A Hospital: No
Multi-Nursing Home (chain) Ownership: Yes
Resident and Family Councils: Both

Magnolia Manor – Inman
Rt 4 Box 1AA
63 Blackstock Road
Inman, SC 29349
(864) 472-9055

Number of Beds:176
Percentage of Beds Occupied: 91%
Medicare Participation: Yes
Medicaid Participation: Yes
Type of Ownership: For-Profit Corporation
Located Within A Hospital: No
Multi-Nursing Home (chain) Ownership: Yes
Resident and Family Councils: Both

Magnolia Manor – Spartanburg
375 Serpentine Dr.
Box 4127
Spartanburg, SC 29305
(864) 585-0218

Number of Beds:95
Percentage of Beds Occupied: 93%
Medicare Participation: Yes
Medicaid Participation: Yes
Type of Ownership: For-Profit Corporation
Located Within A Hospital: No
Multi-Nursing Home (chain) Ownership: Yes
Resident and Family Councils: Resident

Magnolia Place – Spartanburg
8020 White Avenue
Spartanburg, SC 29303
(864) 542-8515

Number of Beds:88
Percentage of Beds Occupied: 97%
Medicare Participation: Yes
Medicaid Participation: Yes
Type of Ownership: For-Profit Corporation
Located Within A Hospital: No
Multi-Nursing Home (chain) Ownership: Yes
Resident and Family Councils: Resident

Mountainview Nursing Home
340 Cedar Springs Road
Spartanburg, SC 29302
(864) 582-4175

Number of Beds:132
Percentage of Beds Occupied: 100%
Medicare Participation: Yes
Medicaid Participation: Yes
Type of Ownership: Non Profit - Corporation
Located Within A Hospital: No
Multi-Nursing Home (chain) Ownership: No
Resident and Family Councils: Resident

Rosecrest Healthcare Center
200 Fortress Drive
Inman, SC 29349
(864) 599-8600

Number of Beds:43
Percentage of Beds Occupied: 9%
Medicare Participation: Yes
Medicaid Participation: No
Type of Ownership: Non Profit – Church Related
Located Within A Hospital: No
Multi-Nursing Home (chain) Ownership: Yes
Resident and Family Councils: None

Valley Fall Terrance, Inc
400 Locust Grove Road
Spartanburg, SC 29303
(864) 503-0377

Number of Beds:88
Percentage of Beds Occupied: 97%
Medicare Participation: Yes
Medicaid Participation: Yes
Type of Ownership: For-Profit Corporation
Located Within A Hospital: No
Multi-Nursing Home (chain) Ownership: Yes
Resident and Family Councils: Both

White Oak Estates
400 Webber Road
Spartanburg, SC 29307
(864) 579-7004

Number of Beds:88
Percentage of Beds Occupied: 99%
Medicare Participation: Yes
Medicaid Participation: Yes
Type of Ownership: For-Profit Corporation
Located Within A Hospital: No
Multi-Nursing Home (chain) Ownership: Yes
Resident and Family Councils: Resident

White Oak Manor – Spartanburg
295 E. Pearl Street, Box 4887
Spartanburg, SC 29305
(864) 585-0241

Number of Beds:192
Percentage of Beds Occupied: 95%
Medicare Participation: Yes
Medicaid Participation: Yes
Type of Ownership: For-Profit Corporation
Located Within A Hospital: No
Multi-Nursing Home (chain) Ownership: Yes
Resident and Family Councils: Both

Woodruff Health Care
1114 E Georgia Road Box 879
Woodruff, SC 29388
(864) 476-7092

Number of Beds:88
Percentage of Beds Occupied: 99%
Medicare Participation: Yes
Medicaid Participation: Yes
Type of Ownership: For-Profit Corporation
Located Within A Hospital: No
Multi-Nursing Home (chain) Ownership: Yes
Resident and Family Councils: Resident

Union County

Ellen Sagar Nursing Home
1817 Jonesville Hwy
Union, SC 29379
(864) 427-5187

Number of Beds:108
Percentage of Beds Occupied: 98%
Medicare Participation: Yes
Medicaid Participation: Yes
Type of Ownership: Government – Hospital District
Located Within A Hospital: No
Multi-Nursing Home (chain) Ownership: No
Resident and Family Councils: Both

Oakmont of Union
709 Rice Street Extension
Union, SC 29379
(864) 427-0306

Number of Beds:88
Percentage of Beds Occupied: 99%
Medicare Participation: Yes
Medicaid Participation: Yes
Type of Ownership: For-Profit Corporation
Located Within A Hospital: No
Multi-Nursing Home (chain) Ownership: Yes
Resident and Family Councils: Both

York County

Beverly Healthcare – Rock Hill
261 S Herlong Ave
Rock Hill, SC 29732
(803) 366-7133

Number of Beds:132
Percentage of Beds Occupied: 98%
Medicare Participation: Yes
Medicaid Participation: Yes
Type of Ownership: For-Profit Corporation
Located Within A Hospital: No
Multi-Nursing Home (chain) Ownership: Yes
Resident and Family Councils: Both

Carolina Village Health Care Center
2993 Van Valin Drive
Rock Hill, SC 29732
(803) 980-8605

Number of Beds:40
Percentage of Beds Occupied: 8%
Medicare Participation: Yes
Medicaid Participation: Yes
Type of Ownership: Non Profit – Church Related
Located Within A Hospital: No
Multi-Nursing Home (chain) Ownership: No
Resident and Family Councils: Resident

Ebenezer Nursing Home
111 Sedgewood Dr
Rock Hill, SC 29732
(803) 329-6565

Number of Beds:99
Percentage of Beds Occupied: 37%
Medicare Participation: Yes
Medicaid Participation: Yes
Type of Ownership: For-Profit Corporation
Located Within A Hospital: No
Multi-Nursing Home (chain) Ownership: No
Resident and Family Councils: Resident

Healthsouth Rehabilitation Hospital
1795 Frank Gaston Boulevard
Rock Hill, SC 29732
(803) 326-3500

Number of Beds:20
Percentage of Beds Occupied: 25%
Medicare Participation: Yes
Medicaid Participation: No
Type of Ownership: For-Profit Corporation
Located Within A Hospital: No
Multi-Nursing Home (chain) Ownership: Yes
Resident and Family Councils: Both

Magnonlia Manor – Rock Hill
127 Murrah Dr.
Rock Hill, SC 29732
(803) 328-6518

Number of Beds:106
Percentage of Beds Occupied: 97%
Medicare Participation: Yes
Medicaid Participation: Yes
Type of Ownership: For-Profit Corporation
Located Within A Hospital: No
Multi-Nursing Home (chain) Ownership: Yes
Resident and Family Councils: Resident

Westminster Towers
1330 India Hook Road
Rock Hill, SC 29732
(803) 328-5000

Number of Beds:44
Percentage of Beds Occupied: 11%
Medicare Participation: Yes
Medicaid Participation: No
Type of Ownership: Non Profit – Church Related
Located Within A Hospital: No
Multi-Nursing Home (chain) Ownership: No
Resident and Family Councils: Resident

White Oak Manor – Rock Hill
1915 Ebenezer Road
Rock Hill, SC 29732
(803) 366-8155

Number of Beds:141
Percentage of Beds Occupied: 99%
Medicare Participation: Yes
Medicaid Participation: Yes
Type of Ownership: For-Profit Corporation
Located Within A Hospital: No
Multi-Nursing Home (chain) Ownership: Yes
Resident and Family Councils: Resident

White Oak Manor York
111 S Congress St Box 629
York, SC 29745
(803) 684-0035

Number of Beds:109
Percentage of Beds Occupied: 99%
Medicare Participation: Yes
Medicaid Participation: Yes
Type of Ownership: For-Profit Corporation
Located Within A Hospital: No
Multi-Nursing Home (chain) Ownership: Yes
Resident and Family Councils: Both

Appendix 2

Resident Measures

(All information was obtained from the Nursing Home Compare Info at www.medicare.gov. This website is produced by **Centers for Medicare & Medicaid Services** 7500 Security Boulevard, Baltimore MD 21244-1850 Phone: 410-786-3000)

Resident Measures

	Percentage of Residents With		
	Physical Restraints (%)	Pressure (Bed) Sores (%)	Unplanned Weight Gain or Loss (%)
Average for all the nursing homes in the United States	9	8	7
Average for all nursing homes in the state of South Carolina	10	10	8
Abbeville County			
Abbeville Nursing Home	9	29	20
Anderson County			
Anderson Area Medical Center Subacute	NA	NA	0
Brookside Nursing Center	24	13	0
Ellenburg Nursing Center Inc.	18	13	2
NHC Healthcare – Anderson	10	5	9
Richard M. Campbell Veterans Nursing Home	0	7	0
Willow Creek Nursing Center	36	11	0
Cherokee County			
Brookview Healthcare Center	18	17	8
Cherokee County LTC Facility	16	12	13
Chester County			
Chester County Nursing Center	18	19	17
Fairfield County			
Fairfield Homes Inc.	10	12	17
Tanglewood Healthcare Center	22	7	7

	Physical Restraints (%)	Pressure (Bed) Sores (%)	Unplanned Weight Gain or Loss (%)
Greenville County			
Allen Bennett Memorial Hospital	NA	NA	0
Briarwood Nursing Center	20	8	0
Brighton Gardens of Greenville	0	16	NA
Fountain Inn Nursing Home	17	7	0
Greenville Memorial Medical Center Subacute Unit	NA	NA	17
Greenville Nursing Center Inc	11	18	4
Laurel Baye Healthcare of Greenville	2	11	5
Magnolia Manor – Greenville	11	13	1
Magnolia Place – Greenville	10	11	4
NHC Healthcare – Greenville	6	10	3
NHC Healthcare – Mauldin	14	4	3
Oakmont East – Nursing Center	3	11	13
Oakmont West Nursing Center	14	8	37
Piedmont Nursing & Rehabilitation Center Inc	9	8	6
Riverside Nursing Center Inc	22	9	1
Roger Huntington Nursing Center	4	7	9
Rolling Green Village Health Care Facility	26	0	23
St. Francis Hospital Transitional Care	NA	NA	4
Stroud Nursing Home	9	4	5
Summit Place, Inc	5	10	7
Westside Nursing Center, Inc	6	17	9
Greenwood County			
Health Care Center of Wesley Commons	15	15	11
Magnolia Manor – Greenwood	1	11	4
NHC Healthcare – Greenwood	3	8	5
Self Memorial Hospital TCU	NA	NA	0

	Physical Restraints (%)	Pressure (Bed) Sores (%)	Unplanned Weight Gain or Loss (%)
Lancaster County			
Lancaster Convalescent Center Inc	6	10	26
Springs Memorial Hospital TCU	NA	NA	0
White Oak Manor – Lancaster	10	10	12
Laurens County			
Laurens County Hospital SNF	NA	NA	NA
Martha Franks Baptist Retirement Center	9	13	21
NHC Healthcare – Clinton	10	6	15
NHC Healthcare – Laurens	3	9	11
McCormick County			
McCormick Health Care Center	17	13	15
Newberry County			
JF Hawkins Nursing Home	18	10	8
Newberry County Memorial Hospital TCU	NA	NA	NA
White Oak Manor – Newberry	13	5	5
Oconee County			
Lila Doyle Nursing Care Facility	10	3	4
Mariner HC – Seneca	13	12	8
Pickens County			
Blue Ridge Nursing Center, Inc	10	8	0
Easley Nursing Center, Inc	14	15	5

	Physical Restraints (%)	Pressure (Bed) Sores (%)	Unplanned Weight Gain or Loss (%)
Harvey's Nursing Home	4	7	7
Laurel Hill, Inc.	29	10	4
Rosemond Nursing Center Inc	11	5	5
Spartanburg County			
Camp Care Inc	1	9	3
Golden Age – Inman	0	7	0
Inman Nursing Home	3	13	11
Magnolia Manor – Inman	26	9	27
Magnolia Manor – Spartanburg	3	3	9
Magnolia Place – Spartanburg	16	9	5
Mountainview Nursing Home	7	5	2
Rosecrest Healthcare Center	NA	NA	NA
Valley Fall Terrance, Inc	28	26	2
White Oak Estates	24	10	14
White Oak Manor – Spartanburg	10	11	18
Woodruff Health Care	0	9	14
Union County			
Ellen Sagar Nursing Home	4	7	20
Oakmont of Union	12	13	14
York County			
Beverly Healthcare – Rock Hill	16	12	20
Carolina Village Health Care Center	NA	NA	NA
Ebenezer Nursing Home	24	24	11
Healthsouth Rehabilitation Hospital	NA	NA	0
Magnonlia Manor – Rock Hill	15	14	4
Westminster Towers	NA	NA	NA
White Oak Manor – Rock Hill	51	15	35
White Oak Manor York	29	8	3

Appendix 3

Inspection Results 1998-2000

(Each symbol or set of symbols beside the numbers represents one incident with a level of harm above 3.)

(All information was obtained from the Nursing Home Compare Info at www.medicare.gov. This website is produced by **Centers for Medicare & Medicaid Services** 7500 Security Boulevard, Baltimore MD 21244-1850 Phone: 410-786-3000)

Abbeville County

Abbeville Nursing Home

Deficiency Category	12/01/2000	11/17/1999	08/06/1998
Mistreatment	0	1	0
Quality Care	4	3*	1
Resident Assessment	2	3	0
Resident Rights	1	0	0
Nutrition and Dietary	1	0	0
Pharmacy Service	0	0	0
Environmental	4	1	0
Administration	1	0	0

*3=Actual Harm: Give each resident care and services to get or keep the highest quality of life possible. Date Corrected: 12/10/99

Anderson County

Anderson Area Medical Center Subacute

Deficiency Category	11/15/2000	11/10/1999	12/21/1998
Mistreatment	0	0	0
Quality Care	1	0	1
Resident Assessment	2	0	0
Resident Rights	0	1	0
Nutrition and Dietary	0	1	1
Pharmacy Service	0	0	0
Environmental	0	1	0
Administration	0	1	0

Brookside Nursing Center

Deficiency Category	09/17/2000	07/09/1999	06/19/1998
Mistreatment	0	0	0
Quality Care	1	4*	1
Resident Assessment	0	0	0
Resident Rights	1	1	2
Nutrition and Dietary	0	0	0
Pharmacy Service	0	0	0
Environmental	3	1	0
Administration	0	2	0

*3=Actual Harm: Give each resident care and services to get or keep the highest quality of life possible. Date Corrected: 9/17/99.

Ellenburg Nursing Center Inc.

Deficiency Category	05/25/2000	02/17/1999	01/22/1998
Mistreatment	1	1	0
Quality Care	3*,^	2	2
Resident Assessment	1	0	1
Resident Rights	0	0	0
Nutrition and Dietary	1	0	1
Pharmacy Service	1	0	1
Environmental	1	3	2
Administration	0	0	0

*3=Actual Harm: Give residents proper treatment to prevent new bed(pressure) sores and heal existing bed sores. Date Corrected: 7/24/00.
^3=Actual Harm: Make sure each resident is being watched and has assistance when needed, to prevent accidents. Date Corrected: 7/12/00

NHC Healthcare - Anderson

Deficiency Category	01/09/2001	01/18/2000	11/18/1998
Mistreatment	0	0	0
Quality Care	0	0	0
Resident Assessment	0	0	0
Resident Rights	0	0	0
Nutrition and Dietary	0	0	0
Pharmacy Service	0	0	0
Environmental	2	0	0
Administration	0	0	0

Richard M. Campbell Veterans Nursing Home

Deficiency Category	09/14/2000	07/08/1999	05/14/1998
Mistreatment	0	0	1
Quality Care	1	4*	0
Resident Assessment	1	2	2
Resident Rights	2	0	2
Nutrition and Dietary	0	0	0
Pharmacy Service	0	0	0
Environmental	3	0	1
Administration	0	0	2

*3=Actual Harm: Make sure that residents with reduced range of motion get proper treatment and services to increase range of motion. Date Corrected: 8/8/99.

Willow Creek Nursing Center

Deficiency Category	07/11/2000	03/16/1999	03/18/1998
Mistreatment	0	0	0
Quality Care	2	2	3*
Resident Assessment	0	0	2
Resident Rights	0	1	2
Nutrition and Dietary	0	1	0
Pharmacy Service	0	1	0
Environmental	0	1	0
Administration	0	0	0

*3=Actual Harm: Give each resident care and services to get or keep the highest quality of life possible. Date Corrected: 4/27/98

Cherokee County

Brookview Healthcare Center

Deficiency Category	12/13/2000	11/16/1999	04/06/1999
Mistreatment	0	1*	1
Quality Care	7	5	2
Resident Assessment	4	6	0
Resident Rights	3	2	1
Nutrition and Dietary	2	2	1
Pharmacy Service	1	2	0
Environmental	4	3	0
Administration	1	6	0

*3=Actual Harm: Keep each resident free from physical restraints, unless needed for medical treatment. Date Corrected: 12/10/99.

Cherokee County LTC Facility

Deficiency Category	04/13/2000	02/26/1999	03/26/1998
Mistreatment	2	0	0
Quality Care	2	0	2
Resident Assessment	0	0	2
Resident Rights	2	0	2
Nutrition and Dietary	0	0	2
Pharmacy Service	0	0	3
Environmental	1	0	2
Administration	1	0	0

Chester County

Chester County Nursing Center

Deficiency Category	07/06/2000	04/21/1999	05/29/1998
Mistreatment	0	0	2
Quality Care	3	2	5*
Resident Assessment	0	0	2
Resident Rights	2	0	3
Nutrition and Dietary	1	0	1
Pharmacy Service	0	0	0
Environmental	2	2	1
Administration	1	0	1

*3=Actual Harm: Make sure each resident is being watched and has assistance devices when needed, to prevent accidents. Date Corrected 7/5/98

Fairfield County

Fairfield Healthcare Center Inc.

Deficiency Category	04/25/2000	02/02/1999	02/19/1998
Mistreatment	0	3*	0
Quality Care	1	3	4
Resident Assessment	0	1	2
Resident Rights	0	3	1
Nutrition and Dietary	1	1	0
Pharmacy Service	0	1	2
Environmental	4	4	1
Administration	1	1**	0

*3=Actual Harm: Protect each resident from all abuse, physical punishment, and being separated from others. Date Corrected: 3/3/99

**3=Actual Harm: Be administered in a way that leads to the highest possible level of well being for each resident. Date Corrected: 3/3/99

Tanglewood Health Care Center

Deficiency Category	08/25/2000	07/01/1999	07/24/1998
Mistreatment	1	2**	0
Quality Care	2*	1	3^^
Resident Assessment	1	1	0
Resident Rights	1	1	2
Nutrition and Dietary	0	1	1
Pharmacy Service	2	1	2
Environmental	4	4***	2
Administration	0	3^	0

*3=Actual Harm: Give residents proper treatment to prevent new bed (pressure) sores or heal existing bed sores. Date Corrected: 9/23/00

**3=Actual Harm: Protect each resident from all abuse, physical punishment, and being separated from others. Date Corrected: 7/30/99

***4=Immediate jeopardy to resident health or safety. Make sure that the nursing home area is free of dangers that cause accidents. Date Corrected: 7/1/99

^4=Immediate jeopardy to resident health or safety. Be administered in a way that leads to the highest possible level of well being for each resident.

^^3=Actual Harm: Make sure each resident is being watched and has assistance devices when needed, to prevent accidents. Date Corrected: 8/31/98

Greenville County

Allen Bennet Memorial Hospital

Deficiency Category	06/14/2001	07/28/2000	09/22/1999
Mistreatment	0	0	0
Quality Care	0	1	0
Resident Assessment	0	0	0
Resident Rights	0	0	2
Nutrition and Dietary	2	1	1
Pharmacy Service	0	0	1
Environmental	0	0	0
Administration	0	0	0

Briarwood Nursing Center

Deficiency Category	02/22/2001	01/26/2000	02/26/1999
Mistreatment	0	0	0
Quality Care	3	1	5*
Resident Assessment	1	0	1
Resident Rights	1	1	0
Nutrition and Dietary	1	0	1
Pharmacy Service	0	0	1
Environmental	0	2	1
Administration	0	0	0

* 3=Actual Harm: Give each resident care and services to get or keep the highest quality of life possible. Date corrected: 5/3/99

Brighton Gardens of Greenville

Deficiency Category	02/02/2001	07/21/2000	
Mistreatment	0	0	
Quality Care	2	0	
Resident Assessment	2	0	
Resident Rights	0	2	
Nutrition and Dietary	1	1	
Pharmacy Service	0	0	
Environmental	0	0	
Administration	1	0	

Fountain Inn Nursing Home

Deficiency Category	08/31/2000	06/15/1999	06/24/1998
Mistreatment	1	0	0
Quality Care	0	4*,^	0
Resident Assessment	0	0	0
Resident Rights	0	2**	0
Nutrition and Dietary	0	0	1
Pharmacy Service	0	0	0
Environmental	0	1	0
Administration	0	1	0

*3=Actual Harm: Give each resident care and services to get or keep the highest quality of life possible. Date Corrected: 7/9/99

^3=Actual Harm: Proper treatment to resident with feeding tubes to prevent problems and help restore eating skills. Date Corrected: 7/9/99

**3=Actual Harm: Inform resident, doctor, family members if resident is injured, major change in resident's health, need to alter treatment, or that the resident must be transferred or discharged. Date Corrected: 7/9/99

Greenville Memorial Medical Subacute Unit

Deficiency Category	02/02/2001	01/19/2000	03/30/1999
Mistreatment	2*,^	0	0
Quality Care	2	4	1
Resident Assessment	1	2	0
Resident Rights	1	3	2
Nutrition and Dietary	2	2	1
Pharmacy Service	0	2	0
Environmental	0	2	2
Administration	1	1	2

*3=Actual Harm: Hire people who have no legal history of abusing, neglecting, mistreating residents or report and investigate any acts/reports of abuse neglect or mistreatment of residents. Date Corrected: 4/30/01.

^3=Actual Harm: Protect residents from all abuse, physical punishment, and being separated from others. Date Corrected: 4/3/01

Laurel Baye Healthcare of Greenville

Deficiency Category	01/25/2001	12/20/1999	12/16/1998
Mistreatment	0	1	0
Quality Care	0	6	1
Resident Assessment	2	0	0
Resident Rights	0	3	0
Nutrition and Dietary	2	4	1
Pharmacy Service	0	1	0
Environmental	1	5	1
Administration	1	2	0

Magnolia Manor - Greenville

Deficiency Category	06/28/2001	05/04/2000	08/05/1999
Mistreatment	0	2*	0
Quality Care	2	5**,^	3
Resident Assessment	0	3	2
Resident Rights	0	5	1
Nutrition and Dietary	0	3	1
Pharmacy Service	2	3	2
Environmental	1	5	4
Administration	0	1	4

*3=Actual Harm: Protect residents from mistreatment, neglect, and or theft of personal property. Date Corrected: 6/11/00

**3=Actual Harm: Give each resident care and services to get or keep the highest quality of life possible. Date Corrected: 7/5/00

^3=Actual Harm: Make sure each resident is being watched and has assistance devices when needed, to prevent accidents. Date Corrected: 6/11/00

Arnold & Arnold, Attorneys at Law

Magnolia Place – Greenville

Deficiency Category	03/24/200	08/19/1999	02/09/1999
Mistreatment	1	0	0
Quality Care	5	4**	6^, ^^, ^^^
Resident Assessment	0	3	2
Resident Rights	0	4***	5
Nutrition and Dietary	0	1	4
Pharmacy Service	2*	0	1****
Environmental	2	2	1
Administration	1	2	4

*3=Actual Harm: Residents are safe from serious medication errors. Date Corrected: 4/17/00

**3=Actual Harm: Each resident is being watched and has assistance devices when needed, to prevent accidents. Date Corrected: 9/18/99

***3=Actual Harm: Provide services to meet the needs and preferences of each resident. Date Corrected: 10/13/99

^3=Actual Harm: Give each resident care and services to get or keep the highest quality of life possible. Date Corrected: 4/27/99

^^3=Actual Harm: Give residents proper treatment to prevent new bed(pressure) sores or heal existing sores. Date Corrected: 3/9/99

^^^3=Actual Harm: Make sure that residents nutritional needs were met. Date Corrected 4/27/99

****3=Actual Harm: That residents are not given too many doses or for too long and make sure that the use of drugs is carefully watched and stop or change drugs that cause unwanted effects. Date Corrected 4/27/99

NHC Healthcare - Greenville

Deficiency Category	01/24/2001	01/19/2000	10/28/1998
Mistreatment	0	0	0
Quality Care	3	0	0
Resident Assessment	0	0	0
Resident Rights	0	0	0
Nutrition and Dietary	0	0	0
Pharmacy Service	1	0	0
Environmental	0	0	0
Administration	0	0	0

NHC Healthcare - Mauldin

Deficiency Category	03/23/2001	02/11/2000	09/23/1998
Mistreatment	0	0	0
Quality Care	2	3*	1
Resident Assessment	1	0	0
Resident Rights	0	0	1
Nutrition and Dietary	0	0	0
Pharmacy Service	0	0	0
Environmental	1	1	0
Administration	0	1	0

*3=Actual Harm: Give each resident care and services to get or keep the highest quality of life possible. Date Corrected: 3/7/00

Oakmont East Nursing Center

Deficiency Category	05/05/2000	03/26/1999	02/25/1998
Mistreatment	0	0	0
Quality Care	5	2	6
Resident Assessment	4	0	3
Resident Rights	0	0	0
Nutrition and Dietary	1	0	0
Pharmacy Service	0	0	1
Environmental	1	0	0
Administration	0	0	0

Oakmont West Nursing Center

Deficiency Category	**05/24/2000**	**01/29/1999**	**02/05/1998**
Mistreatment	0	0	1
Quality Care	3*	3**,^	1^^^
Resident Assessment	1	1	2
Resident Rights	1	1***	3
Nutrition and Dietary	0	2	0
Pharmacy Service	0	0	0
Environmental	2	6****	1
Administration	2	4^^	0

*3=Actual Harm: Make sure each resident is being watched and has assistance devices when needed to prevent accidents. Date Corrected: 6/16/00

**3=Actual Harm: Have enough nurses to care for every resident in a way that maximizes the resident's well being. Date Corrected 2/9/99

^4=Immediate jeopardy to resident's health or safety. Make sure each resident is being watched and has assistance devices when needed, to prevent accidents. Date Corrected: 2/9/99

***3=Actual Harm: Provide care in a way that leaps or builds each resident's dignity and self respect. Date Corrected: 2/9/99

****3=Actual Harm: Make sure that the nursing home area is free of dangers that cause accidents. Date Corrected: 2/9/99

^^4=Immediate jeopardy to resident's health or safety. Be administered in a way that leads to the highest possible level of well being for each resident. Date Corrected: 2/9/99

^^^3=Actual Harm: Give each resident care and services to get or keep the highest quality of life possible. Date Corrected: 3/16/98

Piedmont Nursing & Rehab Ctr Inc

Deficiency Category	12/13/2000	10/13/1999	08/20/998
Mistreatment	1	0	0
Quality Care	6 *,^,**	3	0
Resident Assessment	0	0	0
Resident Rights	2	0	0
Nutrition and Dietary	2	1	1
Pharmacy Service	1	0	0
Environmental	3	0	0
Administration	2	0	0

*3=Actual Harm: Give each resident care and services to get or keep the highest quality of life possible. Date Corrected: 2/14/2001

^3=Actual Harm: Have enough nurses to care for every resident in a way that maximizes the resident's well being. Date Corrected 2/14/01

**3=Actual Harm: Make sure each resident is being watched and has assistance devices when needed to prevent accidents. Date Corrected 2/14/01

Riverside Nursing Center, Inc

Deficiency Category	10/19/2000	08/26/1999	07/29/1998
Mistreatment	1	0	0
Quality Care	1	3	1
Resident Assessment	0	0	0
Resident Rights	0	1	0
Nutrition and Dietary	1	0	1
Pharmacy Service	0	1	0
Environmental	1	2	0
Administration	1	1	0

Roger Huntington Nursing Center

Deficiency Category	06/14/2001	03/30/2000	12/10/1998
Mistreatment	0	1	0
Quality Care	1*	1	2
Resident Assessment	0	0	0
Resident Rights	2	2	3
Nutrition and Dietary	1	1	0
Pharmacy Service	1	1	2
Environmental	0	1	1
Administration	1	0	2

*3–Actual Harm: Make sure each resident is being watched and has assistance devices when needed to prevent accidents. Date Corrected 7/23/01

Rolling Green Village Health Care Facility

Deficiency Category	12/01/2000	11/10/1999	01/29/1999
Mistreatment	1	0	0
Quality Care	2	5*	2
Resident Assessment	5	1	1
Resident Rights	0	1	1
Nutrition and Dietary	1	1	0
Pharmacy Service	0	0	0
Environmental	1	0	2
Administration	0	0	2

*3=Actual Harm: Make sure each resident is being watched and has assistance devices when needed to prevent accidents. Date Corrected: 12/10/99

St. Francis Hospital Transitional Care

Deficiency Category	10/03/2000	12/14/1999	10/08/1998
Mistreatment	0	0	0
Quality Care	1	0	2
Resident Assessment	0	1	0
Resident Rights	0	1	0
Nutrition and Dietary	0	1	0
Pharmacy Service	0	0	0
Environmental	0	0	1
Administration	1	0	0

Stroud Nursing Home

Deficiency Category	08/11/2000	06/04/1999	06/23/1998
Mistreatment	1	0	0
Quality Care	1	0	2
Resident Assessment	1	0	2
Resident Rights	0	0	1
Nutrition and Dietary	0	1	1
Pharmacy Service	0	0	0
Environmental	1	0	0
Administration	0	0	0

Summit Place, Inc

Deficiency Category	06/20/2000	03/19/1999	02/11/1998
Mistreatment	0	0	1
Quality Care	4*	5**	2
Resident Assessment	2	0	2
Resident Rights	2	1	2
Nutrition and Dietary	1	0	0
Pharmacy Service	0	1	0
Environmental	1	1	0
Administration	2	0	1

*3=Actual Harm: Make sure that residents with reduced range of motion get proper treatment and services to increase range of motion. Date Corrected: 6/23/00
**3=Actual Harm: Make sure that each resident's nutritional needs were met. Date corrected: 4/20/99

Westside Nursing Center, Inc

Deficiency Category	08/02/2000	04/28/1999	06/25/1998
Mistreatment	0	0	0
Quality Care	4*	1	3
Resident Assessment	1	1	1
Resident Rights	1	0	2
Nutrition and Dietary	0	1	1
Pharmacy Service	0	0	1
Environmental	2	3	1
Administration	1	1	2

*3=Actual Harm: Give each resident care and services to get or keep the highest quality of life possible. Date Corrected 8/17/00

Greenwood County

Health Care Center of Wesley Commons

Deficiency Category	10/05/2000	05/13/1999	04/14/1998
Mistreatment	0	0	0
Quality Care	3	5	2
Resident Assessment	2	2	1
Resident Rights	0	1	2
Nutrition and Dietary	0	1	0
Pharmacy Service	0	2	1
Environmental	1	3	2
Administration	1	0	0

Magnolia Manor - Greenwood

Deficiency Category	05/23/2001	03/09/2000	03/02/1999
Mistreatment	0	0	0
Quality Care	0	0	3
Resident Assessment	0	0	1
Resident Rights	0	0	1
Nutrition and Dietary	0	0	0
Pharmacy Service	0	1	0
Environmental	0	0	0
Administration	0	0	0

NHC Healthcare - Greenwood

Deficiency Category	01/19/2001	01/13/2000	02/03/1999
Mistreatment	0	0	0
Quality Care	0	0	0
Resident Assessment	0	0	0
Resident Rights	0	0	0
Nutrition and Dietary	0	0	0
Pharmacy Service	0	0	0
Environmental	0	2	0
Administration	0	0	1

Self Memorial Hospital TCU

Deficiency Category	02/09/2001	0/21/2000	04/01/1999
Mistreatment	0	0	0
Quality Care	0	0	0
Resident Assessment	0	0	0
Resident Rights	0	0	0
Nutrition and Dietary	0	0	0
Pharmacy Service	0	0	0
Environmental	0	0	0
Administration	0	0	0

Lancaster County

Lancaster Convalescent Center Inc

Deficiency Category	05/11/2000	02/25/1999	03/12/1998
Mistreatment	1*	1^^	1
Quality Care	6**,^	5	4
Resident Assessment	2***	5	4
Resident Rights	1	3	2
Nutrition and Dietary	3	2	2
Pharmacy Service	0	1	2
Environmental	2	0	2
Administration	2	2	3

*3=Actual Harm: Protect each resident from all abuse, physical punishment, and being separated from others. Date Corrected: 6/5/00

**3=Actual Harm: Give each resident care and services to get or keep the highest quality of life possible. Date Corrected 6/5/00

^3=Actual Harm: Give residents proper treatment to prevent new bed (pressure) sores and heal existing bed sores. Date Corrected: 6/5/00

***3=Actual Harm: Develop a complete care plan that meets all of a resident's needs, with timetables and actions that can be measured. Date Corrected: 6/5/00

^^3=Actual Harm: Keep each resident free from physical restraints unless needed for medical treatment. Date Corrected: 5/3/99

Springs Memorial Hospital TCU

Deficiency Category	04/19/2001	04/13/2000	04/02/1999
Mistreatment	0	1	1
Quality Care	1	1	0
Resident Assessment	0	1	1
Resident Rights	1	0	1
Nutrition and Dietary	1	1	1
Pharmacy Service	1	0	0
Environmental	2	3	1
Administration	0	0	0

White Oak Manor - Lancaster

Deficiency Category	06/12/2001	03/02/2000	01/20/1999
Mistreatment	0	1	0
Quality Care	4	1	3
Resident Assessment	0	0	0
Resident Rights	2	0	0
Nutrition and Dietary	0	1	0
Pharmacy Service	0	0	0
Environmental	2	1	1
Administration	1	0	0

Laurens County

Laurens County Hospital SNF

Deficiency Category	07/13/2000		
Mistreatment	0		
Quality Care	0		
Resident Assessment	0		
Resident Rights	0		
Nutrition and Dietary	0		
Pharmacy Service	0		
Environmental	0		
Administration	0		

Martha Franks Baptist Retirement Center

Deficiency Category	10/24/2000	10/13/1999	11/03/1998
Mistreatment	0	0	0
Quality Care	5	3	1
Resident Assessment	2	1	2
Resident Rights	0	1	1
Nutrition and Dietary	1	1	1
Pharmacy Service	0	0	0
Environmental	1	2	0
Administration	1	2	0

NHC Healthcare - Clinton

Deficiency Category	03/28/2001	02/10/2000	11/18/1998
Mistreatment	0	1	0
Quality Care	3*	1	2**
Resident Assessment	1	1	1
Resident Rights	0	1	0
Nutrition and Dietary	0	0	1
Pharmacy Service	0	0	0
Environmental	1	0	0
Administration	0	1	0

*3=Actual Harm: Make sure each resident is being watched and has assistance devices when needed, to prevent accidents. Date Corrected: 5/4/01
**3=Actual Harm: Provide social services for related medical problems to help each resident achieve the highest possible quality of life. Date Corrected: 12/27/98

NHC Healthcare - Laurens

Deficiency Category	10/05/2000	09/22/1999	08/05/1998
Mistreatment	0	0	0
Quality Care	1	0	0
Resident Assessment	0	0	0
Resident Rights	0	1	0
Nutrition and Dietary	0	1	0
Pharmacy Service	0	0	0
Environmental	0	0	0
Administration	0	0	0

McCormick County

McCormick Health Care Center

Deficiency Category	09/01/2000	07/22/1999	06/25/1998
Mistreatment	0	0	0
Quality Care	2	2	0
Resident Assessment	2	1	2
Resident Rights	1	1	0
Nutrition and Dietary	1	0	1
Pharmacy Service	0	1	0
Environmental	1	1	0
Administration	0	1	0

Newberry County

J F Hawkins Nursing Home

Deficiency Category	08/11/2000	05/20/1999	04/23/1998
Mistreatment	1*	0	0
Quality Care	1**	1	1
Resident Assessment	2***	1	4
Resident Rights	0	1	0
Nutrition and Dietary	0	1	1
Pharmacy Service	0	0	0
Environmental	1	3	0
Administration	2	0	0

* Level 3 = Actual Harm: Protect Resident from mistreatment, neglect and /or theft of personal property. Date Corrected: 10/09/00
** Level 3 = Actual Harm: Give each resident care and services to get or keep the highest quality of life possible. Date Corrected 10/09/00
***Level 3 = Actual Harm: Make sure that a doctor approves a resident's admission in writing and that each resident has a doctor. Date corrected: 10/09/00

Newberry County Memorial Hospital TCU

Deficiency Category	06/21/2000	08/12/1999	
Mistreatment	0	0	
Quality Care	2	0	
Resident Assessment	2	0	
Resident Rights	1	0	
Nutrition and Dietary	1	1	
Pharmacy Service	0	0	
Environmental	1	0	
Administration	0	0	

White Oak Manor – Newberry

Deficiency Category	01/10/2001	12/09/1999	01/05/1999
Mistreatment	0	0	0
Quality Care	0	1	0
Resident Assessment	1	0	0
Resident Rights	2	0	1
Nutrition and Dietary	0	0	1
Pharmacy Service	0	0	0
Environmental	0	0	0
Administration	1	1	0

Oconee County

Lila Doyle Nursing Care Facility

Deficiency Category	05/04/2001	02/25/2000	01/28/1999
Mistreatment	1	0	0
Quality Care	2	3	3
Resident Assessment	1	2	1
Resident Rights	0	1	1
Nutrition and Dietary	1	0	1
Pharmacy Service	0	0	0
Environmental	1	2	1
Administration	1	1	0

Mariner HC - Seneca

Deficiency Category	11/09/2000	08/26/1999	10/23/1998
Mistreatment	2*	1	1
Quality Care	3	6	3
Resident Assessment	3	2	3
Resident Rights	1	0	1
Nutrition and Dietary	0	1	0
Pharmacy Service	1	2	1
Environmental	0	3	3
Administration	2	0	0

*3=Actual Harm: Hire only people who have no legal history of abusing, neglecting or mistreating residents, report and investigate any acts or reports of abuse, neglect or mistreatment of residents. Date Corrected: 12/27/00.

Pickens County

Blue Ridge Nursing Center, Inc

Deficiency Category	01/03/2001	11/17/1999	10/15/1998
Mistreatment	0	0	0
Quality Care	1	0	1
Resident Assessment	1	0	0
Resident Rights	1	1	0
Nutrition and Dietary	1	0	1
Pharmacy Service	1	0	0
Environmental	0	0	1
Administration	0	0	0

Easley Nursing Center, Inc.

Deficiency Category	04/11/2001	02/16/2000	12/16/1998
Mistreatment	0	0	0
Quality Care	0	1	6*
Resident Assessment	1	1	1
Resident Rights	0	2	3**
Nutrition and Dietary	1	4	0
Pharmacy Service	0	0	1
Environmental	0	1	4
Administration	0	0	1

*3=Actual Harm: Make sure each resident is being watched and has assistance devices when needed, to prevent accidents. Date Corrected: 1/25/99
**3=Actual Harm: Provide care in a way that keeps or builds each resident's dignity and self-respect. Date Corrected: 1/25/99

Harvey's Nursing Home

Deficiency Category	01/03/2001	12/17/1999	09/16/1998
Mistreatment	0	0	1
Quality Care	2	3	2
Resident Assessment	3	1	8
Resident Rights	0	1	5
Nutrition and Dietary	0	1	0
Pharmacy Service	0	0	0
Environmental	0	1	3
Administration	2	0	3

Laurel Hill, Inc

Deficiency Category	07/21/2000	08/13/1999	07/29/1998
Mistreatment	0	0	0
Quality Care	0	2	1
Resident Assessment	0	0	0
Resident Rights	0	0	0
Nutrition and Dietary	0	0	1
Pharmacy Service	2	0	0
Environmental	1	0	1
Administration	0	1	1

Rosemond Nursing Center Inc

Deficiency Category	05/17/2001	03/03/2000	02/09/1999
Mistreatment	0	0	0
Quality Care	2	3	2*
Resident Assessment	0	1	4
Resident Rights	1	1	1
Nutrition and Dietary	0	1	0
Pharmacy Service	0	1	1
Environmental	0	3	0
Administration	1	2	0

*3=Actual Harm: Make sure each resident is being watched and has assistance devices when needed, to prevent accidents. Date Corrected: 3/15/99

Spartanburg County

Camp Care Inc

Deficiency Category	07/19/2001	05/02/2000	05/07/1999
Mistreatment	0	0	0
Quality Care	0	2*	1**
Resident Assessment	0	0	0
Resident Rights	0	3	0
Nutrition and Dietary	0	1	0
Pharmacy Service	0	0	0
Environmental	0	1	2
Administration	0	0	0

*3=Actual Harm: Make sure each resident is being watched and has assistance devices when needed, to prevent accidents. Date Corrected: 5/31/00

**3=Actual Harm: Make sure that residents with loss of bladder control receive treatment or service to prevent infections and help get normal bladder control. Date Corrected: 6/5/99

Golden Age - Inman

Deficiency Category	05/15/2001	02/11/2000	02/12/1999
Mistreatment	0	0	0
Quality Care	0	0	0
Resident Assessment	1	0	0
Resident Rights	1	0	0
Nutrition and Dietary	1	1	0
Pharmacy Service	0	0	0
Environmental	4	0	1
Administration	0	0	0

Inman Nursing Home

Deficiency Category	10/04/2000	10/22/1999	12/09/1998
Mistreatment	0	0	0
Quality Care	0	5*,^	0
Resident Assessment	0	4	1
Resident Rights	0	0	2
Nutrition and Dietary	0	3	0
Pharmacy Service	0	0	0
Environmental	0	3	0
Administration	0	0	1

*3=Actual Harm: Give residents proper treatment to prevent new bed (pressure) sores or heal existing bed sores. Date Corrected: 11/19/99
^3=Actual Harm: Make sure that each resident's nutritional needs were met. Date Corrected: 11/19/99

Magnolia Manor - Inman

Deficiency Category	01/11/2001	12/01/1999	09/11/1998
Mistreatment	0	0	0
Quality Care	1	2	2
Resident Assessment	0	1	1
Resident Rights	1	0	2
Nutrition and Dietary	2	0	1
Pharmacy Service	1	0	0
Environmental	3	2	4
Administration	1	0	1

Magnolia Manor - Spartanburg

Deficiency Category	11/15/2000	04/14/1999	04/02/1998
Mistreatment	1	0	0
Quality Care	4*	5	2
Resident Assessment	1**	3	2
Resident Rights	4	3	3
Nutrition and Dietary	1	0	1
Pharmacy Service	5	0	2
Environmental	3	2	4
Administration	4	4	0

*3=Actual Harm: Give each resident care and services to get or keep the highest quality of life possible. Date Corrected: 1/24/01
**3=Actual Harm: Develop a complete care plan that meets all of a resident's needs with timetables and actions that can be measured. Date Corrected: 1/24/01

Magnolia Place - Spartanburg

Deficiency Category	10/12/2000	08/05/1999	05/15/1998
Mistreatment	0	0	0
Quality Care	3	2	3
Resident Assessment	0	0	1
Resident Rights	1	1	0
Nutrition and Dietary	1	1	0
Pharmacy Service	0	1	1
Environmental	0	3	1
Administration	1	1	0

Mountainview Nursing Home

Deficiency Category	10/26/2000	09/22/1999	07/17/1998
Mistreatment	0	0	0
Quality Care	2	0	1
Resident Assessment	0	0	1
Resident Rights	0	0	1
Nutrition and Dietary	0	0	0
Pharmacy Service	0	0	0
Environmental	1	0	0
Administration	0	0	0

Rosecrest Healthcare Center

Deficiency Category	05/23/2001		
Mistreatment	0		
Quality Care	0		
Resident Assessment	0		
Resident Rights	0		
Nutrition and Dietary	0		
Pharmacy Service	0		
Environmental	0		
Administration	0		

Valley Falls Terrace Inc

Deficiency Category	09/14/2000	07/02/1999	05/29/1998
Mistreatment	0	0	0
Quality Care	2	0	2*
Resident Assessment	0	0	0
Resident Rights	1	0	1
Nutrition and Dietary	1	0	1
Pharmacy Service	0	0	0
Environmental	1	0	0
Administration	1	0	0

*3=Actual Harm: Make sure that each resident's nutritional needs were met. Date Corrected: 7/7/98

White Oak Estates

Deficiency Category	10/04/2000	07/22/1999	07/02/1998
Mistreatment	0	1	0
Quality Care	1	4*	0
Resident Assessment	1	1	0
Resident Rights	0	1	0
Nutrition and Dietary	0	1	0
Pharmacy Service	0	1	0
Environmental	0	2	0
Administration	0	1	0

*3=Actual Harm: Give each resident enough fluids to keep them healthy and prevent dehydration. Date Corrected: 8/14/99

White Oak Manor - Spartanburg

Deficiency Category	05/31/2001	03/16/2000	01/27/1999
Mistreatment	0	0	0
Quality Care	1	5	3*
Resident Assessment	0	0	0
Resident Rights	0	1	1
Nutrition and Dietary	0	0	0
Pharmacy Service	0	3	0
Environmental	0	2	0
Administration	0	1	0

*3=Actual Harm: Make sure that residents with loss of bladder control receive treatment or service to prevent infections and help get normal bladder control. Date Corrected: 2/5/99.

Woodruff Health Care

Deficiency Category	09/07/2000	06/18/1999	08/13/1998
Mistreatment	0	0	1
Quality Care	0	1	3*,^
Resident Assessment	0	0	3
Resident Rights	0	0	1
Nutrition and Dietary	0	0	2
Pharmacy Service	0	0	2
Environmental	3	0	2
Administration	0	0	0

*3=Actual Harm: Give residents proper treatment to prevent new bed (pressure) sores or heal existing bed sores. Date Corrected: 9/22/98

^3=Actual Harm: Make sure that residents with loss of bladder control receive treatment or service to prevent infections and help get normal bladder control. Date Corrected: 9/22/98

Union County

Ellan Sagar Nursing Home

Deficiency Category	07/06/2000	04/07/1999	04/03/1998
Mistreatment	0	1	0
Quality Care	2	4**	3
Resident Assessment	0	0	0
Resident Rights	1	2***	1
Nutrition and Dietary	0	1	1
Pharmacy Service	0	0	0
Environmental	1*	1	0
Administration	1	1	0

*3=Actual Harm: Make sure there is a program to prevent/deal with mice, insects, or other pests.

**3=Actual Harm: Make sure each resident is being watched and has assistance devices when needed, to prevent accidents. Date Corrected: 5/4/99

***3=Actual harm: Provide care in a way that keeps or builds each resident's dignity and self-respect. Date Corrected: 5/4/99

Oakmont of Union

Deficiency Category	08/23/2000	05/20/1999	04/29/1998
Mistreatment	3	0	0
Quality Care	7*,^,**,^^	2	1
Resident Assessment	0	4	2
Resident Rights	1	1	2
Nutrition and Dietary	0	0	0
Pharmacy Service	2***	1	2
Environmental	3	2	0
Administration	4	0	0

*3=Actual Harm: Give each resident care and services to get or keep the highest quality of life possible. Date Corrected: 9/20/00

^3=Actual Harm: Make sure each resident is being watched and has assistance devices when needed, to prevent accidents. Date Corrected: 9/20/00

**3=Actual Harm: Make sure that each resident's nutritional needs were met. Date Corrected: 9/20/00.

^^3=Actual Harm: Make sure that residents with loss of bladder control receive treatment or service to prevent infections and help get normal bladder control. Date Corrected: 9/20/00

***3=Actual Harm: That residents are not given too many doses or for too long and make sure that the use of drugs is carefully watched and stop or change drugs that cause unwanted effects. Date Corrected: 9/20/00

York County

Beverly Healthcare = Rock Hill

Deficiency Category	08/24/2000	06/17/1999	07/15/1998
Mistreatment	3*,^	0	0
Quality Care	6	1**	1
Resident Assessment	0	2	2
Resident Rights	5	0	1
Nutrition and Dietary	2	0	0
Pharmacy Service	1	0	0
Environmental	2	3	1
Administration	2	0	0

*3=Actual Harm: Protect each resident from all abuse, physical punishment, and being separated from others. Date Corrected: 9/23/00

^3=Actual Harm: Protect residents from mistreatment, neglect, and/or theft of personal property. Date Corrected: 12/18/00

**3=Actual Harm: Give professional services that meet a professional standard of quality. Date Corrected: 7/1799

Carolina Village Health Care Center

Deficiency Category	**04/05/2001**		
Mistreatment	0		
Quality Care	0		
Resident Assessment	0		
Resident Rights	0		
Nutrition and Dietary	0		
Pharmacy Service	0		
Environmental	1		
Administration	0		

Ebenezer Nursing Home

Deficiency Category	**08/24/2000**	**12/09/1998**	**01/09/1998**
Mistreatment	2	0	2
Quality Care	6*,^	3	4***,^^
Resident Assessment	6	4	5
Resident Rights	1	1	2
Nutrition and Dietary	2	1	1
Pharmacy Service	0	1	2
Environmental	5	1	3
Administration	4**	2	4

*3=Actual Harm: Give professional services that meet a professional standard of quality. Date Corrected: 8/25/00

^3=Actual Harm: Make sure that residents with reduced range of motion get proper treatment and services to increase range of motion. Date Corrected: 8/25/00

**3=Actual Harm: Quickly tell the resident's doctor the results of lab tests. Date Corrected: 8/25/00

***3=Actual Harm: Give residents proper treatment to prevent new bed (pressure) sores or heel existing bed sores. Date Corrected: 3/18/98

^^3=Actual Harm: Make sure that each resident's nutritional needs were met. Date Corrected: 3/18/98

Healthsouth Rehabilitation Hospital

Deficiency Category	**06/12/2001**	**05/25/2000**	
Mistreatment	0	0	
Quality Care	1	2	
Resident Assessment	0	1	
Resident Rights	0	1	
Nutrition and Dietary	0	0	
Pharmacy Service	0	0	
Environmental	2	0	
Administration	0	1	

Magnolia Manor – Rock Hill

Deficiency Category	03/21/2001	03/01/2000	05/13/1999
Mistreatment	1*	0	0
Quality Care	5**	1	1
Resident Assessment	3	1	0
Resident Rights	4***	2	0
Nutrition and Dietary	1	2	0
Pharmacy Service	2	0	0
Environmental	6	3	2
Administration	2	1	0

*3=Actual Harm: Protect residents from mistreatment, neglect, and or theft of personal property. Date Corrected: 4/15/01

**3=Actual Harm: Make sure that residents with loss of bladder control receive treatment or service to prevent infections and help get normal bladder control. Date Corrected: 4/15/01

***3=Actual Harm: Immediately tell the resident, doctor, and a family member if the resident is injured, there is a major change in resident's physical or mental health, there is a need to alter treatment significantly, or the resident must be transferred or discharged. Date Corrected: 4/15/01

Westminster Towers

Deficiency Category	10/17/2000	12/08/1999	09/30/1998
Mistreatment	1	0	0
Quality Care	2	2	1
Resident Assessment	1	0	1
Resident Rights	0	2	0
Nutrition and Dietary	0	0	2
Pharmacy Service	0	0	0
Environmental	0	1	0
Administration	1	1	0

White Oak Manor – Rock Hill

Deficiency Category	11/21/2000	11/02/1999	09/10/1998
Mistreatment	0	0	0
Quality Care	0	0	2
Resident Assessment	0	0	2
Resident Rights	0	0	1
Nutrition and Dietary	0	0	2
Pharmacy Service	0	0	0
Environmental	2	1	1
Administration	0	0	0

White Oak Manor York

Deficiency Category	04/27/2001	02/18/2000	11/10/1998
Mistreatment	0	0	2*
Quality Care	1	0	3**
Resident Assessment	1	0	1
Resident Rights	0	0	0
Nutrition and Dietary	0	0	1
Pharmacy Service	0	0	1
Environmental	0	0	1
Administration	0	0	2

*3=Actual Harm: Protect each resident from all abuse, physical punishment, and being separated from others. Date Corrected: 12/11/98
**3=Actual Harm: Provide social services for related medical problems to help each resident achieve the highest possible quality of life. Date Corrected: 12/11/98

Greenville County

Greenville Nursing Center Inc

Deficiency Category	08/02/2000	05/25/1999	07/07/1998
Mistreatment	0	0	0
Quality Care	1	1	4*
Resident Assessment	1	0	1
Resident Rights	0	0	1
Nutrition and Dietary	0	1	1
Pharmacy Service	0	0	0
Environmental	0	1	0
Administration	0	0	0

*3=Actual Harm: Make sure each resident is being watched and has assistance devices that needed to prevent accident. Date Corrected: 8/03/98

Appendix 4

Nursing Staff Hours

(All information was obtained from the Nursing Home Compare Info at www.medicare.gov. This website is produced by **Centers for Medicare & Medicaid Services** 7500 Security Boulevard, Baltimore MD 21244-1850 Phone: 410-786-3000)

Number of Nursing Staff Hours Per Resident Per Day

	Number of Residents	RN Hours per Resident per Day*	LPN/LVN Hours per Resident per Day*	CAN Hours per Resident per Day	Total Number of Nursing Staff Hours per Resident per day
Abbeville County					
Abbeville Nursing Home	90	.4	.7	2.2	3.3
Anderson County					
Anderson Area Medical Center Subacute	23	.9	.2	2.8	3.9
Brookside Nursing Center	85	.3	.8	2.3	3.4
Ellenburg Nursing Center Inc.	175	.3	.8	2.2	3.3
NHC Healthcare – Anderson	195	.7	.9	3.1	4.7
Richard M. Campbell Veterans Nursing Home	209	.3	.8	2	3.1

	Number of Residents	RN Hours per Resident per Day*	LPN/LVN Hours per Resident per Day*	CAN Hours per Resident per Day	Total Number of Nursing Staff Hours per Resident per day
Willow Creek Nursing Center	57	.4	.9	2.7	4
Cherokee County					.
Brookview Healthcare Center	129	.3	.8	2	3.1
Cherokee County LTC Facility	85	.3	1.1	2.1	3.5
Chester County					
Chester County Nursing Center	100	.3	0	2.7	3
Fairfield County					
Fairfield Homes Inc.	106	.3	.5	2.2	3
Tanglewood Healthcare Center	136	.3	.7	1.8	2.8
Greenville County					
Allen Bennett Memorial Hospital	10	0	0	2.4	2.4
Briarwood	38	.4	.7	2.1	3.2

	Number of Residents	RN Hours per Resident per Day*	LPN/LVN Hours per Resident per Day*	CAN Hours per Resident per Day	Total Number of Nursing Staff Hours per Resident per day
Nursing Center					
Brighton Gardens of Greenville	7	.6	6.9	0	7.5
Fountain Inn Nursing Home	43	.3	.7	2.1	3.1
Greenville Memorial Medical Center Subacute Unit	24	.8	1.3	2.3	4.4
Greenville Nursing Center Inc	77	.4	.9	2.2	3.5
Laurel Baye Healthcare of Greenville	112	.3	.9	2.2	3.4
Magnolia Manor – Greenville	88	.3	.6	1.9	2.8
Magnolia Place – Greenville	108	.4	1.2	1.5	3.1
NHC Healthcare – Greenville	110	.9	1.1	2.6	4
Oakmont East – Nursing Center	126	.5	.5	2.8	3.8
Oakmont West Nursing Center	120	.7	.5	2.4	3.6
Piedmont Nursing & Rehabilitation Center Inc	126	.3	.7	2.3	3.3
Riverside Nursing Center Inc	85	.5	1	1.6	3.1
Roger Huntington Nursing Center	84	.4	.6	2.2	3.2
Rolling Green Village Health Care Facility	31	.8	1.4	1.9	4.1

	Number of Residents	RN Hours per Resident per Day*	LPN/LVN Hours per Resident per Day*	CAN Hours per Resident per Day	Total Number of Nursing Staff Hours per Resident per day
St. Francis Hospital Transitional Care	25	.9	.8	1.7	3.4
Stroud Nursing Home	44	.6	.3	2	2.9
Summit Place, Inc	129	.4	1.6	0	2
Westside Nursing Center, Inc	125	.7	.5	2.8	4
Greenwood County					
Health Care Center of Wesley Commons	96	.4	.7	2.1	3.2
Magnolia Manor – Greenwood	84	.4	.7	2.3	3.4
NHC Healthcare – Greenwood	144	.7	.5	2	3.2
Self Memorial Hospital TCU	10	0	1.3	5.9	7.2
Lancaster County					
Lancaster Convalescent Center Inc	138	.2	.9	2.4	3.5
Springs Memorial Hospital TCU	10	0	1.3	5.9	7.2
White Oak Manor – Lancaster	127	.3	.7	2.1	3.1

	Number of Residents	RN Hours per Resident per Day*	LPN/LVN Hours per Resident per Day*	CAN Hours per Resident per Day	Total Number of Nursing Staff Hours per Resident per day
Laurens County					
Laurens County Hospital SNF	2	.1	8.6	12.9	21.6
Martha Franks Baptist Retirement Center	29	.4	2.3	3.7	6.4
NHC Healthcare – Clinton	117	.3	.7	2.7	3.7
NHC Healthcare – Laurens	155	.3	.7	2	3
McCormick County					
McCormick Health Care Center	119	.4	.7	.7	1.8
Newberry County					
JF Hawkins Nursing Home	98	.5	.8	2.4	3.7
Newberry County Memorial Hospital TCU	8	.2	1.3	3	4.5
White Oak Manor – Newberry	139	.3	.9	2.5	3.7

	Number of Residents	RN Hours per Resident per Day*	LPN/LVN Hours per Resident per Day*	CAN Hours per Resident per Day	Total Number of Nursing Staff Hours per Resident per day
Oconee County					
Lila Doyle Nursing Care Facility	70	.2	.9	2.7	3.8
Mariner HC – Seneca	131	.4	.5	1.9	2.8
Pickens County					
Blue Ridge Nursing Center, Inc	65	.5	.5	2.3	3.3
Easley Nursing Center, Inc	97	.3	1	2.3	3.6
Harvey's Nursing Home	43	.6	.5	2.8	3.9
Laurel Hill, Inc.	79	.4	.8	2.2	3.4
Rosemond Nursing Center Inc	43	.5	.7	2.2	3.4
Spartanburg County					
Camp Care Inc	86	.3	.7	1.7	2.7
Golden Age – Inman	44	.3	.6	1.9	2.8
Inman Nursing Home	37	.4	.6	2.2	3.2

	Number of Residents	RN Hours per Resident per Day*	LPN/LVN Hours per Resident per Day*	CAN Hours per Resident per Day	Total Number of Nursing Staff Hours per Resident per day
Magnolia Manor – Inman	161	.3	.7	2.2	3.2
Magnolia Manor – Spartanburg	88	.3	1	2.5	3.8
Magnolia Place – Spartanburg	85	.3	.9	2.1	3.3
Mountainview Nursing Home	132	.4	.6	2.1	3.1
Rosecrest Healthcare Center	4	.1	3	8.3	11.4
Valley Fall Terrance, Inc	85	.3	.8	2.2	3.3
White Oak Estates	87	.4	1.1	2.7	4.2
White Oak Manor – Spartanburg	183	.3	.8	2.5	3.6
Woodruff Health Care	87	.3	.6	1.9	2.8
Union County					
Ellen Sagar Nursing Home	106	.3	.6	2.1	3
Oakmont of Union	87	.3	.6	2.1	3
York County					
Beverly Healthcare – Rock Hill	130	.3	.8	1.9	3
Carolina Village Health Care Center	3	.2	8	13.1	21.3
Ebenezer Nursing Home	37	.7	.7	2	3.4

	Number of Residents	RN Hours per Resident per Day*	LPN/LVN Hours per Resident per Day*	CAN Hours per Resident per Day	Total Number of Nursing Staff Hours per Resident per day
Healthsouth Rehabilitation Hospital	5	0.7	2.4	1.4	4.5
Magnonlia Manor – Rock Hill	103	.4	.7	2.1	3.2
Westminster Towers	5	.5	8.9	14	23.4
White Oak Manor – Rock Hill	139	.6	.9	2.8	4.3
White Oak Manor York	108	.6	.6	1.9	3.1

*Hours per resident per day is the average daily work (in hours) given by the entire group of nurses or nursing assistants divided by total number of residents. The amount of care given to each resident varies.

Appendix 5

Ombudsman Contact List

Contact List

Anderson, Cherokee, Greenville, Oconee, Pickens, and Spartanburg Counties

Ceila Clark
P.O. Drawer 6668
Greenville, SC 29606
864-242-9733

Abbeville, Edgefield, Greenwood, Laurens, McCormick, and Saluda Counties

Ericca Livingston and Vanessa Wideman
P.O. Box 1366
Greenwood, SC 29648
864-941-8070

Chester, Lancaster, York and Union Counties

Deborah Lewis
P.O. Box 4618
Rock Hill, SC 29732
803-329-9670

Fairfield, Lexington, Newberry, and Richland Counties

Anna H. Harmon and Shirley Smith
236 Stoneridge Drive
Columbia, SC 29210
803-376-5389

About the Author

In 1994, after just two years with a large defense firm, Andy Arnold decided to strike out on his own. This "trial by fire" has made Arnold & Arnold an aggressive team of litigators. Arnold & Arnold represents residents of nursing homes and their families when the resident is injured by neglect and/or abuse.

Andy Arnold is responsible for one of the largest nursing home jury verdicts in South Carolina. He has successfully tried cases in state and federal court and has argued before the Fourth Circuit Court of Appeals and the South Carolina Supreme Court. Brian Arnold, a partner in the firm, has tried cases in both state and federal courts and has nursing home litigation experience.

Andrew Arnold, born Anderson, South Carolina, September 18, 1967; admitted to bar, 1992, South Carolina; 1993, U.S. District Court, District of South Carolina. Education: Spartanburg Methodist College (A.A. 1987); Furman University (B.A.,1989); University of South Carolina (J.D., cum laude,1992). Order of the Coif, Order of the Wig and Robe. Member: Real Property Trust and Probate Journal; National Employment Lawyers Association. Member: American Bar Association, South Carolina Bar. e-mail: aarnold@aalawfirm.com

Brian E. Arnold, born Anderson, South Carolina, July 26,1972; admitted to bar, 1999, South Carolina. Education: Furman University

(B.A.,1994); University of South Carolina (J.D.,cum laude,1999). Order of the Coif, Order of Wig and Robe. Recipient, CALI Award for Employment Discrimination. Editor-in-Chief, ABA Real Property, Probate and Trust Journal, 1998-1999. Member South Carolina Bar. PRACTICE AREAS: Labor and Employment, Nursing Home Litigation. e-mail: barnold@aalawfirm.com

www.ingramcontent.com/pod-product-compliance
Lightning Source LLC
Chambersburg PA
CBHW052244290526
45785CB00016B/1281